PRAISE FOR

A GENTLE PATH OF HEALING

"Debby's insight and intuitive connection with her body and natural surroundings are reflected throughout her work. She dares to ask questions and awaits the answers. Her deep connection with the flow of energy leaves her as a conduit for the power of healing. Her willingness to be vulnerable, with her inner strengths called upon, and her ability to push through fear and pain allows the will of Nature to flow through her. Thank you, Debby, for immersing yourself into the moment—the beauty, the sounds, the smells—of the greatest gift we have been given."

IRENE RIEDL, BS, Ecology and Environmental Technology (EET), LMT, NYS licensed Cosmotologist

"This book contains pearls of wisdom. Debby Havas gently invites readers to experience nature and oneself more deeply and intimately. Her vivid writing and interesting references are inspiring and enlightening. Thank you, Debby, for honestly and caringly offering a guide to enrich life. Following her example, I personally found myself creating unique and beautiful encounters with nature. This is the perfect follow up to her first book, *My Journey to Wholeness*."

DAN SULLIVAN, MPA LMT Certified in Zero Balancing/ 2015 National American Massage Therapy Association Humanitarian of the Year

"Debby's healing story is a wonderful body of ancient knowledge designed in modern language. The fundamental wisdom inside this narrative reminds me of the great teachers of our time, who have said, "How simple life is . . . Why do you complicate it?" Shamans worldwide understand the powerful teachings echoed with-in these pages, and now we all can apply this informative, yet powerful guidance to our own healing journey."

KELLY LINDSAY, Clairvoyant, Astrologer, Past Life Medium, Shaman, author of *Tribal Telepathy* and *How to Read Your Fortune in a Stone*

"*A Gentle Path of Healing* is a vivid, descriptive representation of the relationship between our lives as humans and our natural surroundings. Having experienced profound challenges in her life, Debby elegantly relates how she finds peace, serenity, and comfort in nature, enabling her to move forward meaningfully. The manner in which she explores the breadth and scope of her Adirondack surroundings captures the compelling communion of life and nature . . . The parallels between human life and nature that Debby draws brilliantly synchronize the two. *A Gentle Path of Healing* is a must read for those who are looking for assistance in addressing significant life challenges, as well as for those who appreciate an author's ability to transport readers into the world of nature's beauty and blessings."

DR. PHILIP MARTIN, Former school superintendent in New York State for 38 years, President of the New York State Council of School Superintendents, cofounder and President of the Central New York Education Consortium, and cofounder and President of the Syracuse University Superintendents Alumni Association.

Ed.D., Education Administration, Syracuse University; M.S., Mathematics, Clarkson College of Technology; B.S., Psychology, Rensselaer Polytechnic Institute

A GENTLE PATH OF HEALING

Encountering
Nature's Wisdom and
Curative Energies

A GENTLE PATH
OF HEALING

DEBBY HAVAS

A GENTLE PATH *of* HEALING

Copyright © 2018 by Deborah D. Havas

LITTLE POLLYWOG PRESS
JAY, NEW YORK

Editorial development and creative design support by Ascent:
www.itsyourlifebethere.com

Library of Congress Control Number: 2018902875

ISBN: 978-0-69205-872-5
Printed in the United States of America

for Sara Beth and Wynde Kate
your love for life has served
as my joy and inspiration
every day of my life

CONTENTS

TO MY READERS

I wish to take you on a gentle path—a journey into *my* world, a journey into *your* world. That is, the world of Nature. And may it provide a context for your healing.

I have tried many things to help me heal from Multiple Sclerosis and from other lesser, though still troublesome, ailments. The ones I write about here have worked for me. Maybe they can work for you.

This book is not meant to be a "To Do" list, nor is it a prescription for *your* healing, nor is it a guarantee. We are all different in so many ways, with so many factors contributing to illness and to restoring health. Yet we all want the same thing: to heal in body and in spirit.

Empathy and compassion allow me to understand somewhat where you may be right now. For I have been there also—that state of bewilderment, thinking, *Where* do I begin and *How* do I begin?

This book offers you doorways that can open the path of healing, telling you, simply, what *I* did.

Take away what you will from these stories, the lifestyle changes I made, and the lessons I learned. Through them may you encounter an alternate way that can complement *your* healing experience. Take my words and let them roll around in your head and your heart. Another idea will present itself to you—a place to start, a way to begin.

And you will be off on another leg of *your* journey, your own *healing* journey.

I sought out Nature for answers to my pain and my questions. I asked for insight, for direction. And she had so much to show me and so much to tell.

THE PATH BEGINS FOR ME

It all began for me a long time ago—this long and surprising path of healing.

In 1987, an event occurred that precipitated, and actually catapulted, my journey and my need to heal. Previously, I had been diagnosed with a debilitating disease—Multiple Sclerosis. After the shock of the diagnosis, I was led to begin the painstaking excavation of my traumatic past, releasing the energetic scars left on my psyche. The setting where this took place was the quiet and safety of a northern forest in the Adirondack Mountains of upstate New York. Later, I decided to publish that part of my healing journey in a memoir, *My Journey to Wholeness*.

Yet, I knew my journey was not over. As I took a major step in healing and survival, dealing with issues of the past, I found there was *more* to explore, *more* to question, *more* to understand. Outdoor experiences in the natural world had also contributed very powerfully to my healing of these past issues. Yet, I knew there was still *more* growth to be had, still *more* for me to learn, and therefore still *more* for me to tell.

My diagnosis had thrust me into a whirlwind with no direction. Yet in that whirlwind I discovered a new depth to Nature, though I already thought I'd come to know her quite well. What I think now is that the greater the need you have, the greater Nature's supply for that need. I was very much in need, and so the bounty Nature offered me in terms of her healing energies was just as great.

This book is a collection of personal essays I have been led to write, describing what it is about Nature that I find so healing. Nature is at the forefront. She has continued to be a willing participant and a guide on my healing journey.

I am fortunate to be living in Nature on my property in the Adirondack Mountains. Here I have found the many health benefits that she so willingly provides. While I was involved with the interior work as described in my first book, I also began to wonder what it is about Nature that was affecting my healing in so many ways.

I realize that sometimes in life there are blocks preventing us from opening up and going out in the natural world. Some of us may feel uncomfortable in open space and prefer a more protective environment. Others may experience a fear of being in a forest—encountering a wild animal, getting lost, or being alone. Some people just don't like dirt or insects. Other people may live a distance away from any truly open natural spaces.

Nonetheless, we *can* experience Nature, even in town or city settings, and we can benefit from her healing energies.

I was diagnosed with Multiple Sclerosis at age thirty-eight and had two daughters and a husband at the time. I looked to Nature to find meaning in this new twist on my journey. She helped heal the emotional baggage I had carried for years. As deep as these healings were, I knew there were more to be had.

And will it end? Will my healing ever end?

I await Nature's answer....

I invite you to come along with me on this path—a gentle path of healing.

CHALLENGES

The earth challenges us,
Reaching out to touch us through spirit
With calming, quieting ways,
To counter our stresses,
Relieving us,
Transcending us
To Peace.

My legal separation had been in place for almost the whole year required by our state. I had chosen the condition of living separately and apart for the year, since at the time the state of New York did not recognize irreconcilable differences as grounds for a divorce. During this time, I had many questions, many concerns.

What would be the long-term effect on my two girls? Would they one day come to understand why I had to leave?

And then there was the health insurance issue. The COBRA that covered me for a period of time would eventually cease. What would happen if I hadn't acquired a full-time teaching job by then? How could I afford to buy my own health insurance? And my Multiple Sclerosis could flare at any time, and then where would I be?

And finally, I no longer had any retirement. My husband bought me out of my interest in the family home and, after the mortgage was deducted, I had taken that and invested it at the suggestion of my brother, pretending the money didn't exist. Still, there was a gap in my income.

Would I be able to get a full-time teaching job with the benefits I needed? How long would it take? How many years? It was overwhelming when I let myself think of it all. I had to do something *now*. Get my mind off all of it.

Time to climb a mountain.

But could I ever overcome the great dilemma I faced every single time I set out?

UNCERTAINTY

The sign stood before me, marking the beginning of the hiking trail up Cascade Mountain. Cascade qualified as one of the Forty-Six High Peaks in the Adirondack

Mountains of New York State, with an elevation of 4,098 feet. It held the advantage of being close to Route 73 for easy trail access.

I had dreamed of becoming a 46er twenty-five years before—a 46er being someone who has climbed *all* forty-six of the High Peaks. By climbing one each weekend in decent weather since moving here, I slowly added to the list of peaks I had climbed. Now I was halfway through, and going strong. In fact, I had already climbed Cascade a number of times, and now treated it as a workout in preparation for the longer climbs I still needed to achieve 46er status.

Armed with my backpack and water bottle, I thought I was ready to set out, and I re-checked my day's supplies. *Did I pack everything I might need?* Opening my pack, I saw my headlamp, whistle, guidebook, first aid kit and, of course, my snack. I found mixing up my own gorp worked best for me—peanuts, walnuts, sunflower seeds, and raisins. And, of course, I made sure I had an apple to eat on the top of the mountain. That was part of my ritual. I had made sure to hydrate on my way to the trail, drinking several cups of water ahead of time. I also drank often while I climbed *before* I got thirsty. That way my body could continue flushing the toxins produced by muscular exertion, and I tired less often.

This was a familiar climb by now, one I'd even done after a day of substitute teaching. I looked forward to it now, imagining myself devouring my apple on the summit, resting and watching the sunset before heading down. I hoped that today, like some other days, I would be the only one up on top, because I treasured the time alone on these peaks. It felt like I was sitting on top of the world, with the best possible view.

Standing at the sign-in box, I began to write my name and answer the other questions. *Date? Got it. Number in my party? One. Where am I going?*

With pen still in hand, I hesitated this time. *Summit?* Was that my answer? Even though I'd set out with determination, doubt set in this time. I still experienced some numbness and strange misfirings in my muscles from the Multiple Sclerosis I had been diagnosed with eight years earlier. *Will I be able to make it down this time? Or will my legs give out?*

I had healed in many ways, but the annoying symptoms still moved about my body, seemingly at will. During those times, I could only wait to see if a hand would go completely numb or if a knee would buckle unexpectedly. At those times I didn't feel I could count on my body to support me. I couldn't depend on it. The fear would descend, tightening my shoulders and sending a shudder down my spine. I lived with that fear each day and sought to block it from my mind. I had gotten quite adept at pushing it aside. I rode a fine line between physically doing and overdoing.

I knew that physical exercise was healthy. After all, I had trained as a physical education teacher and had tried to convey that value to my students over the years. My doctor had emphasized that exhaustion while exercising was *not* recommended with this disease and that it could counter any healing attempts my body was trying to make. It was indeed a challenge to ride that fine line between doing and overdoing.

I felt apprehension creeping in again. *What if I get to the top and no one's there and I start to lose feeling in my limbs? I could become stranded. Then what would I do?*

I realized then and there that the biggest challenges can be the internal ones. We can train to overcome physical challenges. How do we overcome inner challenges and limitations? I knew the answer already.

INNER CHALLENGES

You can know *how* to face your challenges. The thing is to go ahead and face them.

I closed the sign-in box and turned the latch, knowing what to do next.

I took a deep breath and slowly exhaled . . . then another . . . and another, picturing my lungs filling with air and then slowly releasing the air. I had learned long before that whenever my old enemy, fear, paid me a visit, deep breathing chased it away.

I had come here with determination, and now, as I continued to breathe deep and let my body and breathing fall into sync with each other, I felt myself regaining not only determination, but also confidence.

Challenge one: Beginning. Conquered!

And once again, I experienced the feeling of assurance that came to me when I was out in Nature, as if no matter what I did, I could not fail.

As I made my way through the lower forest, I recalled the feeling of failure, which I experienced as a sinking feeling in my heart. It was such a frequent sensation in my growing-up years. An expectation of failure had begun in childhood and, as layer upon layer was laid down, my self-image had nowhere to grow but down.

Now, I likened climbing a mountain to making my way through life. It required persistence and determination as the exertion of the climb set in. And it did.

Water droplets formed at my hairline as my body heated, and soon the sweat began to trickle down my spine. My breathing rate increased, and I could feel my heart beating faster and stronger. My eyes were riveted on the roots and rocks beneath my feet as I stepped on, over, and around them, careful to keep from tripping.

The path soon grew steeper, more rutted.

My mind pushed all worries away as I focused on my climbing, aware only of Nature's music surrounding me— the birds calling to each other, the wind passing through the trees, the rush of a nearby stream.

After a bit, I stopped to catch my breath. My eyes began to scan the understory of the forest. I lifted my water bottle to my lips and took a drink of water, feeling the coolness of the liquid as it moved down my throat. Then, with a deep breath, I resumed my climb.

I passed boulders adorned with common polypody, a favorite fern of mine. And wild flowers were visible everywhere. Trout lilies with their yellow blooms and purple-mottled leaves were scattered throughout the woodland. Clintonia with their parallel-veined dark green leaves shown their numerous greenish-yellow flowers, nodding on the long, single stalk to which they clung. Foam flowers with their puffs of white blossoms stood true to their name. All this greeted my eyes as I moved up the mountain and only added to the beauty of Nature's music all around me.

Meanwhile, the nagging thoughts that had risen in my mind earlier kept trying to return. *What if you trip and injure yourself? What if you get to the top and have a flare-up? What if?*

I batted them away like the blackflies that persisted in swarming around my head.

Challenge two: Uncertainty faced and driven away. Conquered!

By the time I neared the top, I was sweating profusely, and my heart was pounding in my chest. My breathing was raspy and quick. *Almost there . . . almost there.* My mind was racing; my focus intent.

And then . . . I broke out of the tree line high up the slope. *Open rock and only a quarter mile to go. I can do it. If I can do this, I can do anything.*

And I knew I could. I had the determination and persistence to figure out my problems. And it would be okay. I just had to keep trying, to be alert and open to new opportunities that were presented. And I had to keep discerning the best route for me to take, both on the hiking trail *and* in my life.

I would make it. I *would* make it.

I have often felt uncertain in my life—uncertain about what to think, what to feel, what to do—as though there was a magic answer, the *right* answer. So how could I be sure of *any* outcome? I had to *experience* something before I could know, in retrospect, whether the choice I made was the best for me. And I realized there was no specific lapse of time for that to occur. Actually, for some things, I might *never* be sure if I had made the best choice.

It was all about fear—fear of the unknown. It was a very stressful state to be in and had been one of my personal stressors for years and, to a lesser degree, still was.

I had also needed assurances from others that I was doing the *correct* thing as if there were only *one* right way—another challenge that still plagued me from time to time.

After reading Pema Chodron's book, *Comfortable with Uncertainty*, I decided there were some ideas I could try. She says, "... instead of always blaming the other, own the feeling of blame, own the anger, own the loneliness, and make friends with it" (p. 185). If I began to feel *uncertain* about a decision and *fearful* of the outcome, I could try to *own* the emotion instead of putting blame on myself or others for it. I could sit with the emotion itself. Over time, it might lessen the intensity. If I could become friends with the emotion and treat it gently, I might regain my previously pleasant demeanor sooner.

Another aspect of my dilemma was my reticence to change. I wasn't comfortable with change, or wasn't until more recently. Change had actually begun to appeal to me. I found it added variety to life; I guess you could say that I *appreciated* change more. Instead of avoiding change, I began to almost welcome it as an adventure, like taking a walk down a winding path through an ever-shifting forest.

My Zero Balancing practitioner, Dan, had told me many times, "Where attention goes, energy grows." Maybe

I *was* becoming more comfortable with appreciating the uncertainties in my life the more I focused on them and the more I sat with them. And where might they lead me? I began trying to look at uncertainty as an adventure with discoveries along the way. After all, "When the student is ready, the teacher will appear." Thank you for your words, Dan.

The nature of life itself is an uncertainty—uncertain as the weather, uncertain as a day in the mountains. I knew I was becoming okay with that—with seeing what is as natural, even as I push my limits against life's conditions.

CLIMBING

Arriving at the peak, I found my favorite spot and sat down. Looking around, I realized no one else was up here.

I was all alone.

And it didn't bother me.

All the fear I had felt creeping in before, all the apprehension about my legs going numb, all of that was long gone. My legs felt fine and so did my hand, not even a tingle. Yes!

Challenge three: Being alone. Conquered!

I had looked my fear right in the eye and overcome it. It could have prevented me from climbing today. Then I would have missed all this beauty that I *viewed* before me and the beauty I *felt inside* of me, too.

I began to realize that *I* was responsible for boosting myself up, and I could do that with Nature at my side. For me it was climbing a mountain that presented the greatest challenge. For someone else it might be taking a hike or clearing all the weeds in the garden. Maybe creating a new path through the woods could be the challenge. Whatever it is that makes us push a little more, risk a little more, discover a little more about ourselves—that's where challenge becomes an ingredient of well-being.

And Nature is there through it all. Nature is the *key* to our well-being. She provides us with the opportunities to learn about ourselves and our special role in this world. That is why we must preserve her. That is why we must protect her.

As I sat there, I began to relax. I felt a swell of pride begin to rise from within. A smile broke out on my face as my breathing became slower and much deeper.

When I was growing up, pride was considered a sin in my family, and both of my parents persisted in squelching any appearance of it in my siblings and me. Since then, I had come to believe that pride is not all bad, and that it is actually a necessary ingredient for well-being to have some pride in yourself.

Climbing is like life to me. I set a goal, accept the challenge, endure the trials, and stick to it until the end, all the time surrounded by Nature. My outer reward is the view I get from the top, but my inner rewards are numerous indeed.

As I struggled to reach the top of Cascade Mountain, with my heart racing and my legs tiring, I felt again that it was all worth the journey. There before me was Nature's vast beauty—the mountains standing as stanchions in hues of green and blue with the sky heralding the beginnings of a setting sun. The sky was becoming filled with a multitude of shades as colors flashed off the clouds, continually dimming and brightening. And I was there to witness it all—just *me*!

I reached in my backpack and pulled out my apple. Sitting there, I let the peace and quiet seep into my bones, into my soul. I felt a rare wholeness of being. Body ... mind ... spirit ... all became ...

One.

After a time, I rose and began my hike down the mountain, carrying with me a peace-filled soul. My problems seemed lessened, or maybe, once again, I had regained a belief that I would figure out what was the best for me. My confidence had been given a much-needed boost.

REWARDED

Long ago I realized that when life happenings and problems get me down, Nature is my catharsis. She is happy to provide us with simple challenges that, if we accept them, provide an opportunity for great reward.

The opposite is complacency, which does not provide for accepting challenges, building pride, and self-confidence. It breeds boredom, negativity, and bitterness. Complacency abhors hard work, setting goals, and the joy of accomplishment. Complacency is accepting the status quo, allowing dullness to overtake the joy of life. Nature is never complacent.

Again, Dan's words came to me: "When the student is *ready*, the teacher will appear." Are *you* ready? Are you ready to go out in Nature and see what she has in store for you today? Are you ready to leave your comfort zone a little and see what happens? Open your eyes and enjoy the lesson....

You won't be sorry.

HEALING ACTIVITY

Climbing mountains has taught me a great deal. Being active out in Nature has kept me in good physical condition as I age. It has helped me continue to heal the emotional baggage I carry from my past. The exercise in Nature, whether I'm climbing a mountain or taking a walk, keeps me focused on the beautiful world in which I live, and allows the worries and cares of adult life in our society to drift away. Problems don't seem as paramount to me when I'm out there. Nature helps me sift through priorities when I'm trying to decide between options. Does this one go along with my values? Is that one the most important? Which is the best choice for me *right now?*

It's where I go to figure things out.

When I'm resting on top of a mountain, I gain a new perspective on things. I get it. I see it. I understand it.

I come away with renewed hope.

I come away believing in myself a little more, and also trusting in the Universe.

I come away with a greater sense of well-being.

Shadows falling at close of day,
Colors drifting—here then away,
Mountains standing so straight and tall,
A journey to the top to follow my call.

A mountain before me,
Many more on the way,
Do I conquer another?
Is that what I do today?

Fear tries to enter
And block it I must,
Apprehension creeps in, yet
In faith, I must trust.

So here at the top,
Sitting quiet and still,
My heart does feel calmed and
My soul does feel full.

The purpose of challenge
Is for my well-being,
For without the challenge,
With fear I'd be living.

And I need to feel whole
From my head to my toes,
Whole in body, whole in mind,
And whole in my soul.

SOLITUDE

U *niqueness*
N *ot loneliness,*
I *nspiring*
T *ruth—*
Y *our Love.*

I close the door on my silver Ford Focus and open the trunk. Grabbing my pack, I'm anxious to set out on my hike today. It's spring and I can smell the comingled scent of thousands of plants and flowers, sprouting and ready to burst with life. The scent of balsam poplar trees mixed with fragrant apple blossoms comes to me. In the forefront of the tree line, I see the apple tree, with its sweet white flowers, crowding the parking area. It's a fresh and clean smell. My lungs fill, and I breathe in newness and life.

I step onto the pine needle-covered path before me.

I turn and enter the forest, noticing the combination of balsam, hemlock, and white pine, branches mingled, coexisting. The day is overcast as the path winds ahead. I walk by glacial-thrown boulders and decaying logs covered with rich green mosses. The sound is stilled, projecting a haunting quality to the atmosphere surrounding me.

The *beep*ing call of a White-breasted Nuthatch breaks the silence. I watch it moving down the trunk of a nearby tree, looking confident and secure on its downward vertical journey. *How do they do that?*

Its pulsing song, as solitary as can be heard anywhere, speaks to me of constancy. Its cadence is as continual as the beat of the human heart, reminding me why I came.

I came to be alone. To step into solitude, and just *be*.

A red squirrel appears out of a bank of just-unfurling ferns and crosses my path, intent on its journey to a nearby tree, bouncing on its way. Then it stops, sits up, and looks my way, utterly frozen. Listening, watching; alert. Then, breaking back into its animated self, it flicks its tail and begins the bantering chatter so characteristic of its species, announcing its displeasure that I am invading its green and growing world.

"Okay," I say. "I'm moving on now."

As I begin to move away, it scrambles over a log and is out of sight.

As I continue walking, I can feel the forest greeting me. My heart slows and my blood pressure drops as I leave the human world behind. All of my personal scrambling and busyness drift farther and farther away with each step I take.

I feel myself becoming alert, senses as heightened as those of the sentinel red squirrel.

The path ahead curves around a large boulder and my sense of intrigue intensifies. *Where is this leading me?*

As I pass the boulder, I can see the softwoods transitioning to a mixture of maples, beeches, and birches. I welcome the fresh green of the forest canopy and its undergrowth. Green is calming and quieting here, although it *can* denote envy or nausea, such as in the saying "he's green with envy." Here, it seems to awaken something positive within me—a doorway opening out from my soul.

Here, I can step out of my own hiding places within and be who I am.

I notice another stand of fiddleheads, beginning to push through the soil, with a blanket of pin-cushion moss that is flaunting its vibrant spring green color. *I wish I knew the names of all the ferns and mosses,* I think.

Turning my head to the right, I can see glimpses of light through the birch trees. *Is that an opening in the woods, or is it water?* I ask myself. The trail I'm walking on is bringing me closer and closer to the light spot.

Water. My pace quickens in anticipation of what I might find ahead.

The path climbs a small hill, with larger evergreens—firs, balsam, a few greening tamaracks—bordering it. As I arrive at the top of the rise, I find myself standing at a large opening, looking over an open lake.

A whole shining body of water lays before me, and before me, at the water's edge, an inviting strip of sand, like a small crescent. The water has the appearance of glass: smooth, unstirred. Not a ripple meets my eyes.

I feel like an explorer. From within, a deep happiness arises and breaks into a smile on my face.

That's how I view my walks in Nature. It's always an adventure, even if it's the same path I travel day after day. To me, it always looks different. Colors change—they lighten, they darken. Plants grow; plants wither. Streams rise; streams fall. The ground is wetter; the ground is drier.

Nature is always changing. It never stays the same. As Augustine said, you can never step into the same river twice.

Or the same forest. Or the same day.

How am I with change? Despite my many years of life experience—shifts, sudden turns, upheavals—do I still resist change?

Nature shows me that change is necessary; otherwise there is stagnation and no growth. Change can be positive; a gift. Yet I am uncomfortable with change. Change provides an opportunity for growth, and I'm all about growth.

So bring on change.

Right.

I remove a towel from my pack. Folding it over a few times, I lay it on the sand strip along the edge of the lake. I seat myself, and in a few moments the stillness that is outside all around me moves inside through that wide-open door of my soul.

I sense myself becoming one with it all, absorbing the solitude—the peace, the quiet, and the calmness of Nature here, today. I feel it suffusing my cells.

Focusing on the water, I notice a slight breeze has begun, as evidenced by the ripples I watch forming.

It's the air's effect on water that causes the ripples—one element responding to another. I think of how people react to one another. How someone's energy can soothe and calm, or stir and lift, or rile and rankle another person.

Here, engulfed in this solitude, I begin to think of love. *Isn't love the highest energy there is?*

I think of love as I watch the ripples gliding toward me—constant . . . continual—until the motion is absorbed. *How do I feel when I absorb love?* I ask myself. *I feel total, complete, filled, even if for just a moment.*

I have experienced many kinds of love. The feeling of friendship is a kind of love, and that feeling can grow stronger in time or not. There's the love for a parent, love for a sibling, a parent's love for their child. There's spousal love. Each is somewhat different, but all are positive. *Are acquaintances a form of love?* I wonder.

There are gradations of love. I might say, "I love apples." That's stronger than saying, "I *like* apples." I "love" you is stronger than I "like" you. Labeling someone as "friend" is stronger than saying she is an "acquaintance".

Caught up in this reverie on the matter of love, I recall the five love languages, which I learned from Gary

Chapman's book, *The Five Love Languages: How to Express Heartfelt Commitment to One's Mate.*

One language is verbal: using words of affirmation such as "I love you," or giving a compliment. Another is physical touch: hugging, holding, squeezing, patting, and sexual love fall into this category. Then there are acts of service, doing tasks to help the other person without being asked. There is spending quality time with the person. And finally, receiving gifts from a person is a way love may be shown.

Many questions enter my mind. *In what ways do I most often show love to another? In what ways do I recognize love being shown to me? And in what ways do I need to have love shown to me?* I spend time with these questions, honestly answering each as I become more aware of myself.

I look above me and view a half-moon still visible in the sky. I keep my eye on it, and it grows lighter as time passes.

I'm startled as I hear a bird call from across the lake, sounding loud and shrill as it travels across the water. Next, I hear the familiar splash as a beaver enters the water from the bank on my left. It seems to be carrying a limb excised from a nearby fallen tree. I'm entranced by its abilities as it maneuvers toward an inlet to the lake.

I bet you're building a dam, I think. *Maybe I'll come back later and see what you've done.*

My gaze surveys the shore and stops at a stand of cattails, standing straight and tall. Their dark brown tails seem to reach to the sky. All of this I see as a gift, my gift of solitude.

A fish jumps in the water, causing bubbles of air to pop to the surface. I watch the ripples of water spreading infinitely, getting smaller and smaller until they seem to disappear. I wonder, *But do they? Or does their energy continue on unseen by the human eye? It's kind of like the words we speak and the effect they have on the human heart. They can hurt and destroy or they can bring a touch of beauty, a touch of love to the listener.* Thoughts ... thoughts ... my mind fills.

> *Solitude, how special you are,*
> *and ... how distant.*
> *yet you lend us your gifts—*
> *uniqueness,*
> *separateness,*
> *seclusion.*

You give them freely but infrequently,
as we fill our lives with busyness
to avoid you,
in fear of what we will discover,
what you will show us . . .
about ourselves.

But if we allow you to enter us,
to take up residence therein,
we find unity in our uniqueness,
unity in our separateness,
unity in our seclusion
from the world.

And then we know—
alone with Nature,
alone with the Divine,
alone with ourselves,
we are whole . . .
once more.

Through experiments using crystal photography, Masaru Emoto has shown that the sounds or vibrations of Nature, which we humans have shaped into words, can affect the crystalline shape of water within our bodies. The shape of the crystals can be changed by the positive or negative words used. In his book, *The Hidden Messages in Water,* Emoto tells us that "The average human body is 70% water" (p. xv). As a fetus, it's 99%; at birth, it's 90%;

during adulthood, it's 70%; and during old age, it's probably about 50%. He concludes that "throughout our lives we exist mostly as water" (p. xv).

Staring at the lake, my mind caught up in facts about water, I think seriously about how what I say to others affects not only their emotions but also their physical bodies. Positive thoughts and expressions promote happiness within our very cells via the water of which they are comprised.

This, I know now, is a key condition for our overall health: to live in a positive space, filled with the energy of love. Words can change the structure of water molecules, and the words "love" and "gratitude" produced perfectly shaped beautiful frozen water crystals, indicating how basic these emotions are to "... life in all of nature" (Emoto, p. 5).

Sometimes when alone, the memories of previous feelings I had of rejection and being unloved, both before and after my diagnosis of Multiple Sclerosis, come flooding back to my conscious mind and seek to drown me once again. But I will not allow it. They do not have any power over me now. They are *only* a memory. It took a lot of work, *hard* work, to uncover the source of those feelings and to heal them. That part of my journey is detailed in *My Journey to Wholeness*.

Now I revel in the solitude and soak up the love I feel being poured out on me and from within me through and by Nature and all the healing gifts that are offered to us.

Do we feel happy when we receive a compliment? What if we heard words of affirmation, support, and praise often? Would we be happier *and* healthier? When someone tells us they love us over and over again, don't we feel great?

And what about gratitude? When we express gratitude for all of Nature's beauty and solitude, the crystalline structure of the water within our body takes on a perfect shape.

I am here all by myself. No other person has come to set foot on this strip of sand. The solitude I find here has brought me to our natural state of love.

And we are whole once more.

LUNAR AND SOLAR ENERGIES

NATURE'S LUNAR ENERGY

My eyelids were still closed, but there was a bright light shining through them—as if I were lying in the sun. Yet I realized it must still be night. Slowly my conscious mind came back on board, and I squinted as I tried to open my eyes.

Slowly, I sat up in bed.

My room looked strange in the moonlight. There was a shadowy presence vaguely outlining my dresser, allowing the rather tall sculpted lamp on top to cast a long shadow across the soft, downy quilt on my bed. The picture on the wall fairly glowed with a fairy-like soft glimmer, while the dark corners of the room held a depth of darkness in sharp contrast to the light.

After a moment, I sank back down beneath the covers. *A full moon.*

I lay there for a while, trying different positions to see if I could get back to sleep. Unsuccessful, I threw back the covers, slipped out of bed, found my bathrobe and slippers, and made my way over to the window. I moved in a daze.

Standing at the window, my eyes adjusted to the brightness, and I could see the moon clearer—every crater. I marveled at the moon itself and the effect its light has on everything.

As a child, I felt a great curiosity about "Mr. Moon" and the "man in the moon," whose face I could sometimes make out. Now, I was just entranced by this potent force of Nature, with its power over the tides, its signal of monthly and seasonal changes.

And that was the thing. I could feel some kind of "pull" now.

Closing my eyes, I remained at the window, minutes passing as I reveled in the bright energy I felt flooding the room.

Soon I felt my limbs and my eyes growing heavy again. I crawled back into bed and began to sink back into sleep, carrying into slumber with me the subtle vibration of lunar energy with which I had just been dosed.

Another evening, around the time of the full moon, I experienced my usual sleeplessness. This time, however, the energies I had been dosed with lasted throughout the following day. I discovered I had experienced a Super Moon and that the moon was the closest to earth it had been since 1948, fifty-eight years earlier.

This time, the increased energies had an unsettling effect on me. I found I couldn't complete *any* task. I'd begin to iron and after only one item, my pile was meaningless. I began a letter and found I'd lost interest in writing. I began to organize some bills and had to stop. For a person who revels in closure, it was a trying day, to say the least.

I felt distracted in my mind, and unfocused. My insides were revved, but I seemed unable to direct the energies present that I had absorbed into my being. I felt that I had accomplished nothing at all. Actually, I had started quite a lot, but had *completed* nothing at all.

By evening, I felt myself begin to settle and my sense of focus reappeared, albeit slowly. I slept well that night, and the following day seemed quite normal for me. It was an experience I will always remember.

I have noticed how the full moon affects me. I am to be counted among the ones who are sensitive to lunar energy. It is not unusual to have sleepless or near sleepless nights around the time of the full moon.

It feels like I am being showered with the moon's energy. I am fully awake and alert. My mind is ready to plan and organize as my thoughts roam around inside my head. It's a time of feeling energized. I might as well get up, because I'm not going back to sleep tonight.

Since I now know that, I use the time wisely. I spend some of the time doing yoga and meditating, setting my intention on healing those in crisis in the world. I also focus my attention on specific people I know who are struggling, even me with my own physical or emotional difficulties at the time.

Send me your healing energy, I think, as I stand beneath her light. *Heal me physically and emotionally.*

I also ask healing for all those who struggle. I ask healing for the world—all the animals . . . all the people . . . all the plants. Protect them with your Light as it shines so brightly overhead.

Then I read or perhaps work on a puzzle until daybreak, something relaxing that I don't normally get to do.

I realize that it's Nature calling me to awaken during those evening happenings. I have learned to give thanks at those times, even though my sleep cycle is being disturbed. I see it as a gift, and a much better gift than any person could possibly give me.

Giving thanks to Nature for allowing me to bask in her gift always helps me to feel better. I am more patient and more loving. I find the more time I spend noticing the delights of Nature, the more positive I feel. Stress does not reside outside my door.

With the setting of the moon, the door closes on another night . . . and a new day awakens.

We had a water well drilled years ago. We sent the water for safe-quality testing. The sample came back as unsafe to drink. We were directed to pour bleach down the well, which we did. Then we let it sit in the pipe for the required amount of time and pumped out the water. The well refilled. We collected a sample of the "new" water. The sample report still indicated that our water was unsafe to drink. We were told by the well driller to complete the procedure again, using double the bleach. Still, the lab report indicated the water was unsafe.

Now what?

When sharing my plight with a trusted friend who works with energy healing, he made a suggestion.

"Take some water from your tap, and let's use the lunar energy to help heal your water."

So, although we were going to be out of town, I opened the faucet and watched the water drain into the glass jar I held directly beneath it. I took the quart of water with me as we drove away. At the time of the full moon, I placed myself outside under its light. For the night before the full moon, the night of and the night after, I performed a ritual. I wrote a prayer for the cleansing of the water in my drilled well.

The year was 2008. The dates were October 13, 14, and 15. I remember that it was quite cold those evenings, so I had to bundle up. I sat in a chair and gently poured the water into a wooden bowl. For ten to fifteen minutes, I dribbled the water through my fingers, over and over. During this time, I spoke my intention, reading from the paper on which I had recorded the words that had come to me so easily.

Universe and Spirit of Words—

This water flows within Your Earth with veins so full and life-giving.

I am grateful for this water, this abundance you have given me, and that which flows within me.

I ask that this water which flows into my drilled well in Jay and all the water within that well be cleansed of coliform and iron bacteria and any other components that might be unsafe for me to ingest. I trust that in time, Your time, all will be set right.

I ask healing of this well water. I believe it to be special and to possess healing qualities for me. Lead me; fill me with Your lunar energy. Let that energy pass through me from this water.

As I am made of water, so let this water also bring healing within me.

As I touch this water, may You touch all the water in that well, the water that is to heal me. Bless this water—all the water. It has been many years in coming to fill our well to overflowing. Let it now be drunk with its sweetness and refreshment for our bodies.

Let it heal us mentally, physically, emotionally, and spiritually.

We rest in the Spirit of the Earth.

May the Spirit of Words carry forth this message to the depths, the source of our well water.

Let it be free ... let it be free ... free to heal ... free to heal. ...

As I prayed, I felt a deep sense of confidence that the water in our well would be cleansed. Every time doubt threatened to intervene, I chased it away, refocusing my intention.

I waited a few days and then took my sample to be tested. The day the letter from the lab arrived, I carried it into my living room and lowered my body into the green stuffed chair I loved. I stared at the envelope, wondering,

What do I do if it's bad news? I held it for a few minutes, doubt warring with faith.

Then I opened it, slowly removed the letter and unfolded it. I could feel my heart beating rapidly. All my muscles were tense. I closed my eyes and took a deep breath. Then, opening my eyes, I focused on the text of the letter.

The water had passed.

"It's clean!" I shouted. "It worked!"

Was it the energy of the moon that cleansed the water? Was it my positive belief that it would happen? Was it my relinquishing *control* over the situation, turning the result over to a power beyond myself?

It was, I believe, a combination of all three.

The Native Americans, among other ancient people, worshipped the moon. They were well aware of the effect it had on germination and growth. Rudolph Steiner, a German scientist, observed, experimented, and developed a program called Bio-Dynamics, by which seeds are planted according to the phases of the moon, coinciding with a lunar calendar. Many people follow this today, myself included. I find the rate of germination to be amazingly high when I adhere to that calendar.

The moon is a powerful source of energy, a force involved in the monthly fertility cycle of every woman on earth. Even the oceans are affected in their cycle of ebb and flow. Isn't it believable, therefore, that it can positively affect our sincere intentions if called upon to do so?

I am reminded of the practice some people have when separated from each other by a physical distance. They feel closer to one another when looking at the moon, for there is only one moon for our planet. Whether they are relatives, close friends, or lovers, the closeness they experience at those times makes it seem as if they are not so far apart.

I have learned much about how to transition my life by living more by the moon's phases. After reading numerous articles on the topic, two of them had what I was looking for ("Lunar Sadhana: Why Women Need to Align with the Moon," Monica Yearwood, www.gaia.com/ article and "Healing with the Moon Energies"; Terry Pippin, thewomensjournal.com/2011/10).

Summarizing their articles, I realize that New Moon is a time to be introspective and to spend more time in meditation. It also presents the opportunity to rest more and delve into the realm of quietude. So I pull back and simplify my life a little. I make simpler meals and spend time journaling. It's a time for me to set my intentions, maybe begin a new project, and possibly renew a relationship.

As the moon waxes, the intentions I have set will gradually gain power. It's a time of building strength and healing, of making more of an effort to protect the environment and ourselves.

At Full Moon, the energies reach their peak and rain down on us. It's a time to ritualize and release any negatives I discovered in my life at New Moon. The idea is to celebrate and honor my energy and accept where I am on my journey.

As the moon wanes, I need to concentrate on any obstacles in my life and release them through a ritual I perform solo.

I feel my peak energies slowly beginning to drift away as I again approach the New Moon phase. I need to set my self-expectations accordingly and not take on additional commitments as the time of New Moon nears.

I have noticed how my creative energies run consistently high for a period of time, as do my physical energies, and yet, for other periods of time, I feel noncreative and physically tired regardless of how much sleep I've gotten. In the past, I neglected to connect my cycle of energy to the moon's phases. Now I know that there is a connection.

Maintaining a hectic schedule at New Moon time would certainly be more taxing on my physical energies and emotional energies and my creative ones, too. But around Full Moon time, energy is present in excess. It is a good time not only to ritualize negatives once and for all, but tap into those energies to finally accomplish my good intentions and bring them to a final peak.

Developing a new idea around waning into New Moon is indeed a struggle for me. Creative energies balk. Yet, waxing into Full Moon, I'm fairly bursting with energy and looking for creative outlets for it. Making a conscious effort to live more in sync with the moon's phases—honoring her by settling down and then rebuilding as she does the same—makes a great deal of sense to me.

In his book, *Yoga & Ayurveda*, David Frawley refers to Ayurveda as a sister science to yoga (p. 5). He writes,

Ayurveda is one of the most remarkable holistic medical systems in the world. It covers all aspects of health and well-being—physical, emotional, mental, and spiritual. It includes all methods of healing from diet, herbs, exercise and lifestyle regimens to yogic practices and meditation. With its unique understanding of individual constitution, Ayurveda provides the insight for each person to create a way of life in harmony both with the world of nature and our higher Self (p. 4).

Ayurveda explains that waxing and waning is ongoing in each woman, in particular, between periods of worldly social contact and periods of self-inquiry. The Shakti *prana*, centered in the womb of every woman, is the source of her strength interwoven with her DNA. It's the seat of her intuitive and empathic qualities. Her emotions flow as the moon waxes and wanes, reaching an emotional high at Full Moon ("Lunar Sadhana: Why Women Need To Align With The Moon," Monica Yearwood, www.gaia.com).

What a challenge it is for every woman in the work world to stay in balance with her natural cycle of harmony, respecting periods of introspection and periods of being socially active.

The moon is a far-reaching source and guide for us to live in conjunction with. The lunar glow affects us, so living in sync with her light phases will augment our living in balance and harmony.

Nature is a wonder.

I recall that there are gardens called moon gardens that consist only of plants that have white blossoms or pale-colored blooms. By day, these gardens can exude a feeling of coolness, yet under the moon these blossoms appear like tiny lights, reflecting the light of the moon. Fireflies dart around, flashing their lights, and moths alight on the white blooms, some of which have opened just for them.

White-blossoming plants are numerous, such as white trumpet daffodils and candytuft, phlox, baby's breath, and cosmos. Some flowers are night-blooming, such as yellow evening primroses; others only release their fragrance during darkness, such as night-scented stock.

Lunar energy is an amazing source of energy that affects our lives each and every day, whether the moon is waxing or waning, new moon or full moon. We are all a part of its cycle. The tides ebb and flow. Plants germinate and grow. Animals respond to their fertility cycles. What would we do without the moon?

Try going out on the next full moon. Soak up the light ... feel the energy.

And give thanks.

> *Full moon, full moon,*
> *Look at you—*
> *Light spots, dark spots*
> *And craters, too.*
>
> *You affect the tides*
> *And plants to sprout.*
> *Germination rings true*
> *And fertility shouts.*
>
> *I wonder what*
> *You'll think of next.*
> *Full moon, full moon,*
> *You need a rest!*
>
> *New moon, new moon,*
> *What do you say?*
> *Do you begin waxing*
> *At all today?*
>
> *The rest you've had,*
> *From you we do learn—*
> *We need a rest, too*
> *From the wage that we earn.*

Soon you'll be full,
Again with bright light,
New moon, new moon,
'Til next month—Goodnight!

NATURE'S SOLAR ENERGY

The fire of Nature—our sun—is, of course, an utterly necessary element, making possible the existence of many life forms on this planet.

The earth's elliptical orbit around the sun is responsible for the changes of seasons that many of us enjoy. As our planet rotates in its orbit around our star, we experience night and day, the hours of nighttime and daytime varying with the seasons.

Plants manufacture their own food with the sun's effect on the chlorophyll in their leaves. They stretch upward to receive the light, their blossoms opening as the sun rises and later closing as the sun sets. With humans, sunlight allows within our skin the formation of vitamin D3, which is an essential ingredient of our health.

Our physical bodies are attuned to the change of seasons. We are drawn to eating more warming foods in the fall and winter—more hot soups and stews. And in spring and summer, fruits and salads help cool us when the temperatures rise.

More and more people are tapping into the sun's energy to heat their homes and to provide the energy needed to run lights in their living spaces and various other uses. Solar energy, our sun's fire, is a continued source of energy for the present and the future.

The spring sun rises in the sky. I open the door and gaze at the brightness of the day: not a cloud in the sky. I feel cheered within, and a smile skips across my face.

As I step outside and close the door, I immediately feel the warmth of the sun's rays—such a change from winter's chill. I move to my wicker chair and sit. Closing my eyes, I feel the warmth penetrate to my bones, deep inside. It is a thorough warming of my*self*. I quiet my mind and open my ears to receive the sound of the birds as they begin to twitter and sing. I feel the wind as it skitters across my skin.

I experience a sense of completeness like no other.

As the world of Nature awakens, so do the energies within *me*. They're rather subtle at first and then rise in intensity as the moments pass, until I can feel them surging to a peak. This is the season where my physical body craves food as my metabolism increases. I am often aware of my stomach grumbling between meals as if I hadn't eaten at all, even though my activity hasn't increased. I feel like I'm feeding a furnace—me—as my body's need for fuel increases to match my metabolic rise.

Spring has arrived.

I was never one to lie on a beach for hours, basking in the sun. My skin rarely burned, but it tanned quite easily. Yet, I found the heat of summer to be broiling and stifling, and so I often escaped to a shaded area. I still find summer's high temperatures to be a bit stifling, causing me, at times, to run from the sun. I also find that the heat drains my energies. Therefore, there are days my status of functioning is minimal. I've just never been a "heat"

person; fifty to seventy degrees Fahrenheit is my ideal temperature range. Yet, I know people who *require* the higher temperatures and, in winter months, need to get away to a warmer climate.

We need our giant star, the sun, to keep us healthy, but too much sun can have detrimental effects. Fields can become scorched, plants may shrivel, and our skin may burn. Solar flares may cause problems not only with transmissions but also our emotions and sleep patterns.

My sensitivity to environmental changes is affected by temperatures above eighty degrees Fahrenheit. Higher temperatures leave me drained and lifeless. Fatigue descends at these times. I am sometimes affected by solar flares—physically, emotionally, and energetically. I struggle with the negative effects the sun has on me. It is my greatest environmental challenge, indeed.

Yet, I have a great deal of respect for this special star, as I observe its gorgeous setting throughout the summer season and feel its awakening warmth in spring. Its "light and bright" effect on me in *every* season lifts my spirit and cheers my soul.

And for that I am forever grateful.

Sunshine, sunshine,
Dancing around,
You make me smile,
Chase away my frown.

I feel your warmth
And bright, bright light,
Encouraging, growing,
Setting everything right.

So what do I do
On a sunless drear day?
When I can't feel your warmth
And your bright light is away?

I go out to Nature
And ask her to show
All the ways your presence
Helps plants here to grow.

And, aha, I do get it,
By hook and by crook.
You're always there watching,
We just have to look.

And lift up our faces
And smile through the rain.
Your bright light and sunshine
We will regain.

TRANQUILITY

What is there about Nature that seems to calm me? Why is it when I am out in Nature, taking a walk or sitting by a stream, everything seems all right even when I know it isn't?

I hurried along the trail toward the sound of water rushing. *Maybe it's a falls*, I thought. *Why am I drawn to water? Tidal waves of water drown and destroy. But doesn't water also cushion us in the womb? Aren't we born of water? Doesn't water have a life-giving quality also— in many ways? Is that why I am drawn to the water—the water of life?*

My steps quickened as did my breathing. I hastened past the briar bushes that bordered the path I was following, their branches heavily laden with ripe luscious blackberries. I gave in to temptation and stopped. Picking a handful, I popped a few in my mouth. I stood there with my eyes closed, pressing the berries against the roof of my mouth. Their juicy sweetness sparked my taste buds. *Delightful!*

I again began my jaunt down the path until it became overgrown with witch hobble which, true to its name, began clawing and clinging to my feet, entangling them in its twining mass. Over I went, head over heels. There I was in its clutches.

The hobble bush is common in the Adirondacks, possibly reaching a height of six feet here. Its limbs grow outward at all kinds of angles, one bush becoming ensconced with the partner beside it until what faces you is a mass of twisted entangled bush. Since this mass of branches can reach a height of six feet, many a hiker has experienced a tremendous slowdown in his or her pursuit of a destination when they encounter the hobble bush community in their path.

As I sat up, I took notice of the brilliant white blossoms

displayed on the bush. I had never seen the hobble bush in bloom before. I fought to untangle myself from the mass. As I rotated my body, I began admiring the blooms a bit closer. Their striking white color seemed magnified against the dark green foliage of the bush. The blooms reminded me of pure white lights, shining their way into my life. Here, in the early spring, they were proudly flaunting their beauty.

I felt kind of glad that I had tripped; my reward was the beauty that surrounded me. *Why was I hurrying, anyway? What was all the rush?*

I picked myself up, brushing dirt and last year's leaves from my pants.

A deep sigh erupted from my mouth. Then I began to step slowly and carefully through the rest of the mass, lifting each foot up high so as to avoid another tumble, still admiring the striking white blossoms. Once through, I began to walk at a comfortable pace, lest I miss another one of Nature's surprises.

I wasn't far away from my goal now. The sound had gotten louder.

Soon I was standing among a thick cluster of speckled alder. The sound was very loud now, and I realized it was coming from just beyond the alders. I stepped forward and carefully separated the branches. There in front of me was the stream whose voice I'd been following, with a number of small falls.

I could feel the energy of the water as it maneuvered over and around the rocks. The water seemed riled and agitated. That same energy transferred to me, giving me an uneasy, all-stirred-up inside feeling. I was seeking peace and quiet ... tranquility ... I *needed* tranquility.

I began making my way upstream. The water seemed calmer the farther away from the series of falls that I traveled. The noise lessened, too.

Finally, I came to a place where the water barely seemed to have any current at all. The surface was glassy and smooth; the entire stream had widened. My inner self resonated with the tranquility of the water at that point. I did not sense any turmoil or agitation or even any disturbance. This is what I had been looking for.

Looking at the water made me feel that there was no disturbance in *my* life, either—that all was peaceful.

Walking farther upstream, I let the sound of the falls drift away until I couldn't hear it at all. I felt so serene and untroubled, so different from the falls with all that energy ... with all that churning and sound.

Shortly, I came upon a grassy area, where I could comfortably sit in a pool of air and light and open space, and just *be*.

Here I was—in the present, neither dwelling in the past nor worrying about the future. Like the tranquil water.

We cannot change the past, and all the "I should haves" do not affect what has happened before this moment. Churning over what is and is gone, what we might have done and didn't, only brings more negative thoughts to mind. We certainly can *learn* from the past and reflect on how we dealt with or didn't deal with past events. Yet, we seem to carry with us the *scars* of these events like canker sores that never go away or that keep reappearing time and time again.

We go on vacation, but do we really relax? Or do we carry with us unhealed turmoil?

I believe the stresses—traumas, hurts, resentments—of living in the past can negatively affect our health if they aren't healed. If we are in need of healing a past relationship, that is certainly worth our time and energy and can even *benefit* our health. *(My Journey To Wholeness*, Debby Havas, pp. 177—218, 275—277.)

I lowered myself onto the soft, green grass. It seemed to absorb my weight and cushion me against the world. The stream I was facing was flowing lazily, meandering its way through the land, in and out with smooth curves. There were willows on the bank, bending their arms toward the stream, drooping limbs almost touching the water.

How healing this place is, I thought, realizing my breathing had slowed and was much deeper. *Something about being in the present and in this deep tranquility was healing.*

An occasional thought came about the bills that were mounting up, about a friend who had betrayed me.

I let each thought rise, as they always will, and just let them go by without engaging them, like leaves carried off by the stream.

Here I can heal.

As I absorbed the tranquility and it absorbed me, my aches and pains faded. I noticed that in some places the water was flowing over rocks, even here, but I didn't hear any sound. The water looked like fingers of silk, skimming over those rocks on its way downstream. I watched it, drifting with the flow.

Time passed.

There at the stream's edge, experiencing Nature's tranquility, any other thoughts gradually left my mind. Nature was all there was, and I was a part of Nature. And peace rang through it all.

In perhaps an hour, I roused myself a little from my reverie and arose. Slowly, I began making my way back to the path that brought me here, back to the falls.

Turning around once more, and with a parting glance at the stream, I took a deep breath, inhaling the air, the quiet, the scene poised before me held in stillness, eternity, unfathomable peace.

I am rejuvenated once more, I thought, as I focused again on the return path. The stillness lingered with me as I glided down the path with the sound of the approaching falls gradually breaking into my consciousness.

I began to realize, as I moved along, that I *had* found an answer to my question, the one I had asked myself at the beginning of this hike: Why was I always drawn to water?

Now I knew ... because I had again been touched by it within my very soul.

Water gives life ....
Water sustains life ....
Water is life.

Tranquility—quiet and calm are you,
Physical pain seems to disappear,
The turmoil in my life is gone,
Nature's gift is here.

You free us from the past we've lived
And worry is far away,
A desire so deep—to truly be
In the present is the place.

The presence you hold and we attain
Through experiencing your gifts anew,
Free from disturbance our body feels
The peace we never knew.

BEAUTY

Anyone who keeps the ability
to see beauty never grows old.
—Franz Kafka

I stand under a sugar maple tree in the fall and watch the orange and yellow leaves drifting down around me. I inhale the scent that identifies the season. Standing there, I begin to ponder: *What is beauty? Why are our spirits so uplifted—a great factor in healing—when we are in the presence of beauty?*

Is beauty found in a certain mix of colors and hues we see as we sit at the edge of a lake watching the sky that's painted with a spectacular sunset? Or is it in the design or pattern the colors make as the sun reflects off the clouds?

Do we sense beauty in the feel or texture of a velvety soft green blanket of moss? Or find it as the scent of a fragrant flower we stoop to smell while wandering through a garden?

Is it the intricacies of the sparrow's nest, with each blade of dried grass intertwined with another? Or is it the rhythmic movement of the waves as they lap at the shore of the lake?

Is it the sparkle of a spider's web, glistening with dew in the dawn of a new day? Or is it the melodic voice of a Rose-breasted Grosbeak, calling from its perch in a nearby birch tree?

Is it the metamorphosis of a butterfly as it leaves its gold-laced chrysalis? Or is it the cry of a newborn babe at the moment of entry into our world?

Is it the *feeling* we get when we witness something beautiful? Is it a place of awe—a rainbow after a summertime shower, a full moon rising on a crisp and cold fall evening?

The beauty of Nature surrounds me at all times. I see it. I feel it. I hear it. I smell it. I touch it. Nature's beauty engulfs me, envelopes me, enfolds me in its exquisite presence. And all my worries dissipate, fading outward like ripples on the water.

Colors aglow -
The setting sun hovers,
Kissing the earth "goodnight,"
Pulling a blanket over the world—
Beauty.

Rachel Carson once wrote, "Those who contemplate the beauty of the Earth find reserves of strength that will endure as long as life lasts" (www.wiseoldsayings.com). And my experience is that those reserves of strength *will* see us through our difficult times.

Spending time in Nature provides that opportunity to absorb her beauty. Gazing at the spider's intricate glistening web or watching the sun setting on the horizon, amidst an array of dazzling color, we are stronger . . . we are healthier . . . we are happier.

There is beauty in creation, always, however concealed at times either by natural blight or by our darker moods.

Beauty confronts the ugliness in our lives. We have brokenness. We have pain. We feel anger and hatred, jealousy and envy. We experience sadness. We experience grief. If we can rise above the ugly emotion and notice the beauty surrounding us and the beauty living within us still, we are able to relax and allow ourselves to absorb the beauty. Beauty is a salve for that ugliness that has soaked into us.

Beauty is a Presence even amidst our pain.

Walking out my door one day, I saw a feather lying on the ground before me. It was small and brown, quite non-descript. There were no special markings on it or anything to help me identify it. Was it a wing feather? I stooped to pick it up, placing it in the palm of my hand. It nestled there quite nicely.

I brought it closer to my face, examining my find. *What a marvel*, I thought. *What kind of a bird are you from?*

It felt so soft and smooth as I gently stroked it from base to tip. I could feel the strength in it and stood amazed at its design; it was like a tightly woven piece of fabric with each thread attached to the next. Together, the threads provided a solid network of waterproof protection.

How perfect it was, how utterly perfect in every way. The shape was oblong and curved, while the coloring was gradual, the light brown shading to a darker hue as my eyes moved toward the tip. As I slid my fingers across it in a caressing motion, it felt like a piece of silk.

Some would likely have stepped over it as they hurried on their way or even stepped on it, giving it no mind. But I saw beauty in it. To me it was a gift—a connection with the beauty of flight and color and with the sense of uplift. I turned around and carried it back inside.

I have a shelf in my home that I call my Nature Shelf. There I keep the little surprises, the gifts Nature leaves for me every day. I can sit down and look closer at my find in the evening, discovering Nature's message for me. *Am I open enough to read it today, or am I clogged with worry and anxiety?* Nature takes my mind off my problems for a spell and sometimes shows me a solution. She is always there for me.

THE "BOOK OF NATURE"

To me, feathers represent growth and change. For the bird, perhaps, a time of molting, and for us humans, a shedding of the present and an opening for the new to be created.

Besides feathers, my Nature shelf contains eggshells dropped by dutiful parents after the chicks have hatched, as well as various bird's nests.

When I look at the nests that have dropped from trees, I see birth, growth, flight, and a return to birth as new eggs are laid. In a few weeks, a bird has changed and become ready to live on its own, while parents work day and night to feed and protect it and teach it survival skills. Isn't that what *we* also do?

> *In this nest, Mother lays eggs,*
> *In this nest, babies are born.*
> *In this nest, they grow and grow,*
> *In this nest, scars are formed.*
>
> *In this nest, young birds feed,*
> *In this nest, they are kept warm.*
> *In this nest, young birds rest,*
> *In this nest, they weather the storm.*
>
> *In this nest, they cry for Mother,*
> *In this nest, they wiggle and squirm.*
> *In this nest, they fight and smother,*
> *In this nest, what is it they learn?*
>
> *From this nest, it's time to leave,*
> *From this nest, ready or not.*
> *From this nest, they fly away,*
> *From this nest, to another spot.*
>
> *From this nest, they travel afar,*
> *From this nest, with all they have learned.*
> *From this nest, yet an embryo in flight,*
> *From this nest, the emptiness still burns.*

From this nest, instinct will carry them,
From this nest, they will find their own way.
From this nest, they will survive,
From this nest, 'til another day.

Beauty can be as small and as seemingly insignificant as the tiniest grain of sand, irregularly shaped and coarse to hold. Or it can be as vast as the horizon of trees aglow with a shimmering glimmer on a moonlit night.

I don't have to *see* beauty for it to exist, for I can *feel* beauty, also. It makes me feel balanced. Everything seems right in the world. I feel grateful, thankful, and uplifted by beauty as if my body has been given the gift of flight and I'm off, soaring high above the forest. It energizes and inspires me to go on living my life, searching for the truth, *my* truth, my purpose here.

Beckoning fingers
Pulling me into being one
Within its arms—
> *engulfing,*
>> *embracing,*
>>> *enfolding me to its own.*
A spiritual presence—
> *Beauty.*

Is it what we see *and* what we feel, what we smell *and* what we touch, as we experience beauty? And what about what we hear? Can't that have beauty, also? I have heard it said that beauty lies in the eyes of the beholder, but I feel beauty goes much deeper than in just seeing it.

Beauty is the initiator of a feeling deep within. It's a connecting link to something greater than us. It's a lifeline of love in circular time.

I watch Nature flow in circular time. The earth revolves on its axis, while the planets revolve around the sun. The pathway of a swimmer's arms move in a circular pattern, propelling her forward. The head of a sunflower traces the sun's seeming movement throughout the day. A pebble tossed in the lake radiates concentric circles throughout the water. A tornado's funnel of forceful winds and a whirlpool's downward pattern of spinning water are ever present. The rings inside a tree trunk allow us to count the years of growth. The shell of a snail and the form of a bird's nest are circular in shape.

Nature abounds in cycles, and a cycle has no end. There is birth, life, death, and decay, yielding new life. Seeds germinate, sprouting with vigor and growing, blossoming, and yielding seeds to begin the cycle again. Water is a liquid present in a lake that evaporates, forming water vapor. Clouds are created as the vapor condenses, finally returning to earth again in liquid form as rain.

Another cycle involves the lifelines of love that are planted in a person when we give our time to them. The positive feeling they receive from us moves to them and through them to another. It gets returned to us either directly from that person as the sharing of their response with us or from someone else at another time. Lifelines of love have no end. They travel around and around, through us and back to us, over and over again. Isn't that another form of beauty?

At times, beauty brings me to tears. It may be the look of total innocence in a child's eyes or the look of pure delight.

To touch beauty is to touch the Universe. I tell my grandchildren that Grandma cries "happy tears" as they watch them trickle down my cheeks when I view a rainbow or feel the gentle spring rain. I am far from sad.

And I ask myself, *Where would I be without beauty?*

Fall gives way to winter, and I realize every season gifts us with its beauty.

As snowflakes drift downward, landing on my nose and eyelashes, my face breaks into a smile.

As a child, I remember opening my mouth, awaiting the ice-cold landing that would tell me I caught a snow-flake right on my tongue. And then, like a snap of my fingers, it would melt away. What fun! I would try to catch another . . . then another . . . and another. It would some-times tickle when one landed on my eyelashes, and I'd laugh right out loud. Hours would pass while I ran around catching snowflakes on my face and feeling them touch me like so many kisses, light and delicate. Every one of them fleeting.

Beauty can bring delight.

Then there was the wonder of frost on the window—swirls and bursts and shattering patterns of white, each more intricate and beautiful than the next, like danc-ers on the stage. I would feel a small ember within me catch fire as I stared at Nature's handiwork on the glass, knowing that in a few moments, the sun would touch and dissolve it.

Beauty can bring wonder.

Now, I look at the snow piled up from a recent snow-fall and I see a sea of diamonds winking at me over and over again. And I know . . . I have seen beauty and I have felt beauty.

As Martha Reben tells us in her personal tale, *The Healing Woods*, the wilderness gave her "... a sense of the freshness and the wonder which life in natural surroundings daily brings and a joy in the freedom and beauty and peace that exist in a world apart from human beings" (p. 250).

After reading her story of healing outside in the Northern woods, I come away with the thought that whatever our illness or condition is, the more we focus on it, the more power we give it in our lives. And we get worse. If we are depressed and we concentrate on all the ills we have, we can think of even more, and pretty soon *everything* is depressing in our life.

If we look around at Nature in all its beauty, we can lift that depression. Focus on Nature, not on our ills, and we'll feel a lot better.

Look at Nature. Listen to Nature. Touch nature. Feel Nature. Smell Nature. She's there for us to use to heal. Go out and visit her. She will surprise you.

Spring brings thirst-quenching showers, as young plants vie for new growth and strive to survive. Spring holds the beauty of rebirth and renewal as Nature awakens from its wintertime rest. It reminds us that we need periods of rest also, for aren't we a part of Nature?

How often do I take the time to rest? I tend to be a person who always has something to do; yet, I have learned that rest is necessary and should not be looked at as being lazy. Our body needs rest, as does our mind. I function much better and am more able to use my personal gifts when I am rested. And I am not to feel guilty about it.

Rest does not necessarily mean sleep, but it may. Rest means being relaxed, open, and taking time for ourselves away from necessary jobs or tasks. That's the key word: *necessary*. Of course, we all have responsibilities, and life throws many challenges our way. But clearing our mind can give our body the rest it needs. I have found that a walk in Nature does that for me. Something else that helps me is engaging in the practice of yoga. The practice goes back over five thousand years. It addresses our physical body by stretching and strengthening as we attain various positions, or asanas. Mentally, through the quieting of the mind, we find we can control our thinking. And our soul finds nourishment through the meditative aspect of the practice—a body, mind, and spirit connection for sure.

We can feel Nature's beauty even *inside* our home. Besides my Nature Shelf, I can use the principles of Feng Shui to give me a more calming, peace-filled, and pleasant domicile where beauty reigns. The Chinese practice of Feng Shui "... identifies conditions in a living space that affect us in either positive or negative ways. According to Feng Shui, the language of an environment tells a story, and if we change the elements of our surroundings, we can improve the story" (Nancilee Wydra, *Feng Shui: The Book of Cures*, p. 13). We are talking about the flow of chi.

In her book, *The Feng Shui Garden*, Gill Hale explains what is meant by the energy called chi. "Chi is the invisible essential life force present in every form of life in the universe. Where it flows freely and accumulates, there is health and abundance. Where it stagnates, there is sickness and decay" (p. 32).

The use of color and placement corresponding to the bagua has helped me a great deal. This was first explained to me through a VHS tape I purchased. The copyright was 1999, and it was published by Feng Shui Productions L.P. It was called *Feng Shui: Creating Environments for Success and Well-Being*. The presenter was Grand Master Lin Yun, the spiritual leader of the Black Sect of Tibetan Tantric Buddhists and a leading authority on Feng Shui at the time. He and Feng Shui expert Deborah Gee gave an explanation and demonstration of Feng Shui principles that I found easy to understand and easy to begin using. That's when I began to change around my furniture placement and moved appropriate colors into areas of my rooms. As I did so, I began to notice a difference.

The rooms felt more uplifting as I opened up areas where the flow of chi was more natural. I eliminated the blocks, and the increase in positive energy in the room was evident. I noticed I could think better, and I felt sharper, more alive, and happier.

The placement of each color and of pieces of furniture in our home can have a positive or negative effect on our emotions and, therefore, our health. The principle consideration is not to impede the flow of chi but to allow it to flow freely.

I open my front door and step inside. I'm caught by a flash of red on the wall facing me—a painting of a forest of red maple trees. What a greeting! Immediately, I feel bright and energized.

I look to my right, where I have placed framed pictures of my family on the windowsill. A smile crosses my lips as I view the cheerful faces of my children and grandchildren looking back at me. It gives me a warm, comfortable feeling.

As I look to the left I see the comfortable stuffed chair I've placed there, covered in green fabric. When I see the color green I think of plants and growth and the vibrant nutrition of green vegetables. An important element to have represented on the left side of the room is wood, and that's exactly what the base of my chair is.

As time has progressed, I've extended my use of the bagua to the corners of my room. The placement of furniture and an emphasis on element and color has given my home a more comfortable happier feel.

Let the chi flow!

The beauty of summer is the warmth of rising temperatures. The budding trees have opened to lush green leaves. Now the sprouts of spring give way to the growth of summer, and blossoms produce future seeds. But too much heat can dry the plants and shrivel the blossoms.

Two forces always present.

Too much of anything destroys the beauty, even the beauty of love. Many a relationship is destroyed by power and control. The possessive tendency of too much love wreaks havoc with the heart. And too much power seeks to stifle the gifts of the one controlled. Love is an energy that can build up or break down the beauty within.

Two forces always present.

Can you recall the energy you experienced when you fell in love? It was boundless—excitement, anticipation, expectancy, and thrills. There was no end to it. That same amount of energy surrounds us in summer.

The forest takes on a darker tone as limbs become covered by leaves and the canopy thickens. The bright shafts of light we got used to in spring are now filtered out as we walk.

Summer's beauty has a solid quality of constancy and growth as we watch trees grow another foot in height and see the consequent changes that take place in the undergrowth. *What changes do I encounter as I grow? What effect do those changes have on those around me?*

The beauty of summer is strong and constant. I hear the wind through the white pines and I am lulled to sleep, only to be awakened in the morning by the Mourning Dove calling outside my window.

> *The seasons hold a magic thread*
> *That spins the whole year through.*
> *Listen and see,*
> *Touch and smell,*
> *Nature's scent is there for you.*
>
> *Fall is the fragrance of falling leaves,*
> *Winter's the feel of icy cold snow,*
> *Spring is the sprouting*
> *That we see,*
> *And summer—the winds that blow.*

The seasons come, the seasons go
And so our life goes on,
The beauty we see each day
And each night
Will be our lasting song.

Nature speaks to me of beauty. There are the animals, the plants, the wind, the rain or snow, the sun, the moon—all aspects of Nature as I walk along in the forest or sit in the quiet, alone in my reverie. I soak it up. I absorb it into my bones, my soul. And I feel whole, complete, at peace.

In my home, I turn on a small water fountain and listen to the gurgling of the water as it moves over the rocks in the bowl that is part of the fountain.

A stone, a feather, a grain of sand, a plant, a picture of forest or falls—all of this helps me when I am feeling worried and anxious and am unable to take that walk or immerse myself outside in Nature. I just sit down in my chair and close my eyes, visualizing beauty and pulling it into my very soul. I revel in the calming of my being. Time passes by. I resist all pressure and allow myself to feel the healing touch of beauty.

We sprout, we grow, we blossom, and we wither as our own life cycle comes to its end. We are ever present with Nature. Where *would* we be without her?

"Remember," I tell myself aloud, "there is beauty within *me*, also. I carry *that* wherever I go. I share it with the world."

SOUNDS AND
FREQUENCIES

Many now claim that sound has a healing aspect. Does it? What about Nature's sounds?

No matter where we are, whether in city or country, Nature's sounds surround and support us. There is birdsong, the sound of the wind, rainfall. Beyond sound, there lies a deep silence that has its own quality. Yes, Nature's sounds are present everywhere.

In the stark, scientific sense, sound is the result of a vibration of air falling on the ear, loud and jarring or soft and comforting. But it is much more than that. Sound evokes memories and triggers responses from our physical being and spirit.

I make it a personal, healing habit to walk outside, especially in the early spring, to catch the birds' musical notes. There is something fresh and new and life-affirming in their warbles, chirps, and trills. Each song has a different melody made up of different tones in different patterns at different tempos. Yet, it all blends so beautifully. I feel myself enmeshed and uplifted in the whole, great web of *life*.

There are songs only sung in the spring as part of courting rituals. Then there are songs sung when the eggs have hatched and the fledglings are encouraged to fly. There are the songs of mature adults, greeting the sun as it breaks over the land at dawn. Other songs warn of danger from intruders like the shout of the Blue Jays, echoing throughout the forest. I associate these sounds with nurture and protection.

Different birds seem to sing at different times of day. In the morning, I hear the Mourning Dove and Indigo Bunting, while near evening, the Brown Thrasher announces the close of day. Others we hear only in the night, such as the owls that awaken at that time of day to hunt and feed and, of course, the Whip-poor-will. When I was a child, I lay down many nights to its repetitive tones as I drifted off to another world. I know that life has its beginnings and endings, and all are part of Nature's plan.

Traveling down a back road in Jay, New York, and parking amidst the apple trees that were growing there was the setting of my first encounter with the call of the Great Horned Owl. How poignant and stark it sounded in the twilit shadows. Yet, I was filled with such peacefulness that I didn't want to leave. It conjured up feelings and thoughts of mystery. When I hear the owl call, I allow myself to rest in the great mystery of it all, not needing everything to make sense, or for every question to have "an answer".

Evening finds me sitting on a boulder at the edge of a lake near my home. No movement stirs the air. The call of the Common Loon penetrates deep within my being—so forlorn, yet in harmony with our wilderness surroundings. I feel at peace as the vibration of its call lands on my ear and goes deep—all the way to the center of me. And I know no matter where I am, regardless of how I may feel, in Nature I am never really abandoned and alone.

SOUND HEALING AS A MODALITY

Nature has many sounds that provide us with the opportunity to heal. Think of the rhythm of the ocean waves as they break upon the shore—constant and continual tones. Is it the rhythm that is so hypnotic? What about the vibrations that are set in motion by the force of water? What about the sound itself—the notes, the pitch? Doesn't that transfer to an experience of bliss within our very soul? Or if we sit by a gurgling brook—how does that make us feel? Calmed, relaxed? How does that happen? *Why* does that happen?

I think of birdsong and how their different calls blend into a beautiful chorus of sound. I have never felt upset by listening to birdsong. That's one thing I love about being outside. The songs of the birds never seem to interfere with one another. And I detect no competition among them for the *loudest* call. Volume doesn't seem to matter—the softer calls are just as important as the stronger ones. The blended quality of sound is amazing. They each seem to lend their gift to the chorus. And yet how many times have you been in a group of people where there seem to be a few who need to increase in volume, as if that makes everyone else listen to *them*, as if they are the most important?

The sound of the wind passing through the white pines—I can fall asleep just listening to it. There's no specific rhythm, just vibration of air as it moves through the pine boughs, getting louder and softer as air currents change. And I drift with it, so relaxing . . .

I think of peepers in the spring and crickets chirping in the fall. The note is the same, over and over again. The rhythm doesn't change. It's all repetitive, constant, unchanging. The tempo is even, yet it can lull us to sleep.

In her book, *Tuning the Human Biofield*, Eileen Day McKusick introduced me to the principle of entrainment. I now understand that if we hear two different tones, one by each ear, the difference between them is what our brain hears. If the difference is a frequency of 10 Hz—the Alpha brain wave range—we will experience relaxation.

Is that what's happening with Nature's calming and peace-filled sounds? Is that why we can get lost in them, be carried away by them? Is that why Nature's sounds seem to improve our mood and reduce our stress?

Why we can fall asleep to them? Is our brain actually becoming entrained by the combinations of tones our ears receive?

Nature has placed the opportunity for healing at our fingertips. We need only to recognize the gifts she offers, respect them, partake of them, and be thankful for them. She asks nothing more of us in return. It's up to *us* to protect and preserve them.

UNCOMFORTABLE SOUNDS

Some sounds make me feel uncomfortable, such as the sounds made by frozen water—ice.

The loud, sharp, cracking sound of ice moving on a frozen pond, expanding as it forms more ice, is not a healing sound to me. Fear overtakes me at that sound. It makes me feel unstable, unsure, and very miniscule in the scheme of things. The startling pop of it makes me jump.

A roaring waterfall elicits a similar reaction from me. It extracts fear, and my muscles tense, my heart quickens, and my blood pressure rises. I feel a contraction within.

Air makes sounds, also. Strong winds are louder. The air vibrates more, and the force is greater.

Louder winds cause me to tense up inside. I live in a valley, and my home is on the side of a mountain, bordering that valley. I lie awake during a nighttime windstorm, listening to the rushing torrents of air traveling through. As it picks up speed, it begins to moan, increasing until it reaches a dull roar that keeps building until I'm sure a tree is going to come crashing down on my home. The trees bend and sway with the greater vibration of the wind until it passes and moves up the valley, its sounds dying away in the distance. My heart slows its beat and my blood pressure resumes a normal state. I unclench my teeth, and I drift off to sleep.

Fire is another one of Nature's sounds. The roar of a forest fire would not be a healing sound, in and of itself. The destruction and "out of control" quality causes fear and intimidation, humbling us in its wake. The initial destruction is devastating, yet, Nature has her own healing quality and, *given time*, a new forest will regenerate. Nature *can* reclaim herself—the factor is time. How long will it take? And that assumes no human interference.

The earth itself makes sounds that strike terror within me. The thought of tremors, earthquakes, and aftershocks unnerve me. The tremors I have heard cause me to tremble. They are of one tone—a kind of moan as everything shudders and shakes. I feel scared at those times and, therefore, tense and constricted within, my heart beating wildly as I anticipate the ending. Will there be another? Will it become an earthquake this time? What will I do? It shakes me to the core.

Then there are sandy banks on streams that erode and collapse along with rockslides. Trees are uprooted during storms and come thundering down, having been ripped from their anchor. These are not healing sounds for me.

Sometimes a sound causes me a lot of anxiety or frightens me. It creates a feeling of not being safe. When that happens, I try to calm myself by moving to a place I feel safer. Then I close my eyes and take some slow, deep breaths. Sometimes it takes a while before my heart stops racing and my breathing returns to normal. When this happens, though, I feel much better. Sometimes I feel the need to cry afterwards. I take a walk in Nature and allow her to help me understand why I feel so much anxiety and maybe what I can do to prevent a reoccurrence. I take my time—I watch, listen, and just breathe.

HEALING SOUNDS

I have quite a different reaction to pond waters.

The still water in a pond elicits a feeling of solitude and tranquility, while gently flowing water allows me to feel calmed and pensive. There is an inner expansion and relaxation that takes over. Rushing water exudes more energy and inspires me to action.

It's the amount of energy the sound elicits that determines its healing effect for me. The less the amount of energy, the slower the flow and, therefore, the quieter and more gentle the sound. For me, there is more opportunity for the healing capability of sound at slower and lower vibrations.

I find the gentle wind quite healing. I let it blow through my hair, making me feel unencumbered by anything or anyone. I find myself floating in the present moment, the here and now. My mind is absent of all thought.

I just am.

The crackling of a campfire, spitting and sparking, elicits feelings of camaraderie and aloneness—an individual among friends. I feel warmed, comfortable, and safe. The fire is mesmerizing as I stare at it. As it begins to die, I rise and stir it, watching it come to life again with a flame that grows higher and higher—kind of like life—disappointing and then reenergizing. The flame soon disappears and reappears in a different spot by a different log. The heat warms the molecules, creating more vibration and causing the air to spark the fire in different places.

The crackling sound of the campfire is pleasant to my ears. It is the healing sound of unity, and I am one with it all.

Another healing sound for me is the sound of digging in the garden with my trowel, planting seeds, or the sound of children building sand castles at a lakeside beach.

I find moving sand with my hands or feet to be quite soothing. The sand may be saturated or perfectly dry. I become lost in the feeling of it as it moves through my fingers or toes.

Making designs in the sand or drawing pictures in it calls me back to the present, and I am here, now. As I move the sand, no other thoughts enter my consciousness. There is only room for the sensual experience of moving sand.

SOUND SENSITIVITY

I have become aware of and am fascinated by the crackling frequency emitted by tree roots, which scientists have been able to measure at 220 Hz. This was reported in *The Hidden Life of Trees* by Peter Wohlleben (p. 13). He refers to the research done by Dr. Monica Gagliano from the University of Western Australia and her colleagues, who have been studying the communication between plants. It was also observed that the plant's root tips oriented toward this frequency when they were exposed to it.

Health practitioners have told me that each organ of the body has a different vibrational frequency, and that the measurement of the vibrational frequency of the lungs is also 220 Hz. It makes me wonder if this communication at 220 Hz in trees is an impetus for transpiration—the movement of water from the roots up through the plant to the stomata of the leaves. It collects on the underside of the leaves and evaporates from there. I've sometimes seen the droplets on tree leaves and bushes while walking. The carbon dioxide in the air is absorbed through these same stomata. Then, in the presence of chlorophyll, the carbon dioxide combines with the water and sun to produce glucose for the tree, and oxygen is released into the air.

This is called respiration and produces the oxygen we need for life. Is it possible? Is this how the tree "breathes"? We need each other to survive—plants and us.

More discoveries are yet to be had in this field, and I suspect Dr. Gagliano and her colleagues will offer us more in the future.

As each of the organs in the human body vibrate at a different frequency from the other, so do each of the *chakras*—the energy centers in the body. Each *chakra* center vibrates with the same frequency as a specific color (the colors of the rainbow), and closely corresponds to a note on the musical scale (www.mysticbeats.com/The-Chakras.php).

The *Root Chakra*, for example, vibrates with the same frequency as the color red and closely corresponds with the musical note of C. If we are struggling with the feeling of insecurity, we might wear a red shirt or place a red scarf around our neck. We might watch a red sunset or help ourselves to a bowl of strawberries. Think *red*.

Musically, the note C closely corresponds to the *Root Chakra*. Traditional Hatha Yoga and Ayurveda would use a *mantra* LAM (or Lum) for issues involving the *Root Chakra*, intoning the note of C. More familiar to most of us is the musical scale beginning with *do* and finishing with *ti* for the *Crown Chakra*. These syllables may also be used for intoning while we repeat the *mantra*.

Colors, *chakras*, and musical notes all have corresponding frequencies. The vibrations around us can affect our mood and our stress level. It's possible this is why some of us feel uncomfortable entering a room painted vibrant red or orange or when hearing heavy metal music. Our own healthy vibration and that of each organ within our body is being challenged and thrown out of balance. If this happens long enough, illness or disease may result. This is the thinking behind the field of sound therapy, the principle of which has been used for thousands of years. Treating the *chakras* or any part of our body with vibrations or sound frequencies can bring it back into balance. Intoning with the musical scale using our own voice could also aid in this process. And then there are the sounds of Nature, herself, allowing us to relax, calm down, and just *be*, calling us back to what *is*.

The fact is, Nature wants to communicate with us, and our bodies, minds, and souls respond to her various languages. Our bodies respond by feeling calmed and relaxed; blood pressure drops, heart rate decreases.

Our minds respond by quieting from the worries that plague us. The unending questions that keep hammering our minds are replaced with the healing sounds of Nature. Or maybe there is only healing *silence* to be heard. Our souls respond by being uplifted. We feel a freedom from the burdens that cause such heaviness within; emotional healings of hurts from the past transpire.

ADDING OUR VOICE TO NATURE'S

What happens when we speak words of kindness, care, and love?

When we are hurting, when we are grieving, the sincere words of another can help to ease our pain. Whatever trauma we have experienced is an opportunity for another to express kindness and caring. It might be the words that are spoken, the physical touch of the hand on our arm, the hug that is offered, the written words in a card received—these are the languages *we* use.

Carrying our burdens to Nature and voicing our needs to her, chanting a mantra, or intoning sounds brings a connection with her, as our voices blend and she offers us back a healing blessing. The love we express to one another is the healing love that Nature offers to us each day.

As in Dr. Masaru Emoto's research on frozen water crystals in *The Hidden Messages in Water*, our words and the sounds or vibrations our words produce can affect the water present in the makeup of another person, plant, or animal. The most beautifully perfect crystal created was from the words "love and gratitude" (p. 5).

Sounds are indeed a healing energy of Nature, whether the vibrations are caused by moving air, flowing water, the heat of a campfire, shifting sands, singing birds, or the human voice. Think of that the next time you become aware of the sound of water flowing or the sound of the wind moving through the trees, or when you hear the sound of your own voice.

And think—Love.

Water, Fire, Earth and Air
Are elements around us here.
To help us, heal us on our way
To show our love to all this day.

GROUNDING

Solid, stable, a sense of place
A connection—safe and secure,
When I'm grounded to you, Oh Mother Earth,
Your Presence is assured.

Why is it that I love to walk on the beach in my bare feet? The sand can be wet or dry; it doesn't seem to matter.

When it's wet, I like the amazing sensation of the sand oozing between my toes. It squishes up and covers them as I stand at the water's edge. I sink into the drenched, loose sand until it reaches my ankles. Then I pull my feet out and continue my walking.

I like to leave footprints in the wet sand like I'm the first one to make a trail here. Actually, I am . . . today.

The water erases all trace of my presence as it quickly fills in my print. So onward I go to make another . . . and another . . . and another.

I feel so safe and secure, walking along the beach, or sitting on a rock, or lying on the ground. It's a feeling of "place"—kind of like being "at home," even though the house where I sleep is miles away.

I feel stable in my physical body and my emotions seem quite even.

In *Tuning the Human Biofield*, Eileen Day McKusick writes:

> The surface of the earth has a negative polarity, and the bottoms of our feet have a positive polarity, and through this interface we exchange electromagnetic energy. Most people wear shoes all day, and because the soles are insulators, they never have the opportunity for energy exchange. There is a theory . . . that much of the inflammatory issues that plague the population are the consequence of a buildup of ungrounded electromagnetic energy in our bodies (p. 172).

McKusick explores the science of sound and its use therapeutically. She discusses the biofield and using it in combination with the *chakras* in sound healing. Ultimately, she discusses the use of tuning forks in adjusting the frequency of the vibration in that part of the body and thereby healing it. A fascinating book.

I am reminded of how I feel after a Zero Balancing session. Zero Balancing is a healing therapy that reorganizes us energetically from the inside out. It relieves stress and tension, aligning energy with structure and penetrating bone deep. It was developed by Fritz Frederick Smith, MD. He combined his experiences as an osteopathic doctor with his training in cranial osteopathy, yoga, meditation, Taoism, Eastern teachings on energy medicine, and becoming a master acupuncturist, and Zero Balancing was born. The result was an effective sequence of moves, applying pressure at the joints and vertebrae. This method identifies energetic or structural imbalances, releases tensions, and encourages them to vacate the body. This allows balance to return (*Zero Balancing Bridging the Mind and Body Through Touch;* Zero Balancing Health Association).

After my zero-balancing session, I always experience a feeling of evenness. Everything seems right in my world. I feel grounded. Any discomforts I had when I arrived seem to disappear, whether emotional, psychological, or physical. My outlook is brighter, and I am blessed with a great deal of patience for many days, a sure sign to me that all is in balance once again.

When I feel grounded, I know I can handle whatever comes my way. No matter what the situation, I have confidence that it will all work out. And it always does somehow.

I have a solid feeling when I am grounded. It brings to mind my experience of sitting on the rock on top of Porter Mountain in the Adirondack Park in New York State.

As I sat there one summer day, I could see my life before me. Was I becoming dependent on my two daughters for the love and affection I was missing from my marriage? Or worse, was I, in turn, encouraging *their* dependency on *me*? Was I *discouraging* their *independence* instead of encouraging it?

It was time to sort out my responsibilities as a parent, their guide. My girls were *not* my possessions. I began to see my priorities in a healthier light. Ways to encourage their independence came to mind. I knew what I needed to do next.

Being grounded, sitting on this rock in the wilderness, brought a connection to Nature. Things seemed to fall into place for me right then.

I came away with a new focus, a healthier focus. I felt my mission had shifted from continuing to breed dependence *on* me to beginning to breed some independence *from* me. I could allow more decision making on their end and integrate more opportunities for them to make their own choices.

It was time for me to pass along my new and healthier focus to my girls. Being grounded had allowed me to do that.

Clinton Ober, in his book *Earthing*, speaks of Matteo Tavera, a French naturalist. Tavera has written about our connectedness with Nature and feels that our health will be better if we reconnect with Mother Earth, along with eating more wholesome, chemical-free food and breathing clean air. In Taveras's book, *La Mission Sacree*, he says that we have insulated ourselves from Mother Earth by building floors that isolate us and by wearing footwear made from unnatural materials. Therefore, our electrical connection is slowed, resulting in an increase in chronic illness.

Tavera sees, according to Ober, that our main purpose is to carry the electricity through our bodies from the earth to maintain a balance of health (*Earthing*, p. 22). He suggests possible ways of reconnecting with Mother Earth: going barefoot, exposing our skin to natural water, sitting or leaning against the trunk of a tree. Then we will reap the benefits of a better mood, a healthier state, and a joyful demeanor (*Earthing*, p.23). That is his message.

Clinton Ober worked on the early development of programming and marketing for the cable and communications industries, and he discovered that his sleepless nights improved, as did his severe chronic pain, when he grounded himself to the earth. He details his story in a book called *Earthing*, written by himself, Stephen Sinatra,

M.D., and Martin Zucker. It explains how, when we become disconnected with the earth, there is more opportunity for disease to develop in our body.

Ober theorized that there is an analogy between the human body and cable TV. The cable has many channels flowing through it. So does the body in the form of nerves and blood vessels conducting electrical signals. When grounded, the body is not disturbed by the environmental electrical interference of electromagnetic fields and static electricity. Without direct contact with the earth, the body is continually being charged (p. 34).

He felt this continual charge was causing his sleepless nights and severe chronic pain. His story is worth reading, as it relates how he pursued proving that what he was experiencing himself was a true health discovery.

Here's why.

The earth has a magnetic field that resonates with a vibrational frequency. The closer and more often we can come to that frequency, the more in balance we are. But our culture has turned away from what our Native American ancestors knew.

Our footwear is no longer made from natural materials like animal hide. Man-made vinyl and plastic have replaced even rubber. We don't move around barefooted very often, and when we do, it's on painted concrete or carpeting. We choose to disconnect with Mother Earth by putting a block between us. Our bare real wood floors have become laminate in our homes. We've grown beyond the dirt floors of long ago, but have we really grown at all? Have we thought to replace the dirt with something else that still connects and grounds us?

If what the authors of *Earthing* say is true, then the way most of us live is disconnected from the Earth. And, therefore, we are out of balance most of the time.

I wonder if that's why I love walking on the sandy beach, sitting on a rock, and lying in the grass. . . . I need to feel connected to the Earth.

RECONNECTING

There are ways to connect even when we can't walk barefoot. I found that using a grounding pad while I was seated each day helped to alleviate the energy drain I experienced with my diagnosis of Multiple Sclerosis and even afterwards. In addition to that, I began using a seat pad in my car for the same reason.

My "grounding pad" is placed beneath my bare feet

when I'm seated at the computer or watching a movie. "The pad uses a metallic fiber mesh and conducts coupled to a wire connected to a ground outlet in the wall . . ." (*Earthing*, p. 104). Since electrical systems have to be grounded for safety purposes, I am grounded while sitting *inside* my home with my bare feet resting on my pad. It doesn't use electricity; it only uses the ground to connect me with the earth, allowing me to resonate more closely with the earth's vibration and, therefore, to be more in balance.

I have an "auto seat pad" in my car that is a smaller version of the grounding pad. It helps to relieve my tension and fatigue while I am driving or riding in my car. The pad connects by an insulated cord with a metal clip attached. I clip it on an unpainted metal part of my vehicle. Paint renders it not as effective. It blocks the connection to the earth.

I find the metal frame of my seat works well for me. I simply scraped off the paint in one place and always connect it there. I am semi-grounded through the metallic mesh I am sitting on to the metal frame of my car.

I have found an increase in my energy level and, therefore, an increase in the number of hours I can drive or ride before fatigue sets in. The EMFs (electromagnetic fields) are very strong in a concentrated space such as an automobile where we are seated for hours at a time.

When I began using a computer, I noticed I could only work on it for ten minutes before I was exhausted. That's when I began researching EMFs and their effect on health. I started to find out how I could protect myself. Being grounded helps me tremendously to both relax and stay balanced while maintaining my energy supply.

The Earthing Institute and EarthCalm are two resources that have used technology to develop devices that protect us when we are exposed to too many EMFs and also devices that help to ground us when we can't go barefoot. I have used them for myself and in my home, protecting me from the large amount of EMFs being produced by our cell towers, computers, cell phones, iPhones, tablets, and so on, while connecting me to Mother Earth. I still use my grounding pad in my home and seat pad in my car.

The more time I spend grounded and connected to Mother Earth, the more balanced I become. The more in balance that I am, the happier I am and the more my gifts flow outward to others.

Just as the earth has an electromagnetic field, so do we. Some refer to it as our aura. I have found that if I am exposed to too many EMFs at once, I experience a huge energy drain and feel empty and lifeless. My ability to concentrate is affected, and so is my memory. I don't seem to have the energy to function at all.

For that reason, I wear a necklace with a protector built inside to help combat the EMFs I'm exposed to when I leave my home. EarthCalm inventor, Jean Gallick, developed Living Earth Technology after thousands of experiments over a period of thirty years, resulting in the technology used in the Nova Resonator necklace and other EMF protection products. Each one serves to "enhance a person's grounding in the electromagnetic field of the earth and restore the body's immune system," promoting deeper levels of healing (*The Ultimate EMF Protection;* Earthcalm).

In my home, I have a scalar unit in one of my outlets that protects everyone from the EMFs coming off any electrical devices. There are also small rectangular pads that adhere to any wireless devices—laptops, tablets, cordless phones, iPhones and cell phones—when they are not plugged into any outlet.

As our electro-smog increases, so does our vulnerability to stress. With the development of advanced technology, we also have people who are using technology to develop ways to protect us from its side-effects, which can affect our health and that of our children in future years.

We each have our own electromagnetic field or aura. Mine is quite large, and so I am prone to picking up others' problems or difficulties as they pass through my field without knowing it. Consequently, I become drained very quickly in crowds or malls. Knowing that about myself, I am cautious about where I go and how long I remain in areas where many people gather.

I can be sure my aura is cleansed afterwards by doing some visualizing. I picture myself standing under a waterfall and feeling the water wash away any negative energy that I may have come in contact with and that has attached to me.

I also use techniques to pull in my aura *before* I enter a crowded place where I'm apt to be exposed to many auras. I would use them before entering an airport, for example.

One way is to stand with my eyes closed before entering the crowded area. I picture a beautiful rose in the air in front of me. I focus on the beauty of it and then gradually move it over to my left side and then picture it behind me. I continue slowly moving it around to my other side and then above my head. Finally, I move it beneath my feet. I breathe slowly and deeply during this activity, always focusing on the beauty of the rose. I may repeat this any number of times as practicality, appropriateness, and time allow. This helps me tremendously to maintain my energies at a functioning level, especially when away from home.

Another cause of energy drain is environmental factors. I have found that a change in air pressure can initiate a headache. Using my Neti Pot seems to relieve those symptoms so much that I don't have to take painkillers. If I need to go out and be civil among people, a natural anti-inflammatory like quercetin with bromelain seems to do the trick. Pineapple is a great natural source of bromelain. I try to use a natural remedy for any discomfort I experience, if possible. That way I find my body is more accepting of it without side effects.

I seem to be sensitive to earthquakes above 6.0 on the Richter scale that occur anywhere in the world. I feel very logy on those days and a few days afterward, depending on the severity of the quake. At those times, I cut back on any demands that would drain my physical energies. I might postpone an appointment and reprioritize my schedule, taking more time for relaxing and grounding activities. I figure if the Earth needs to borrow some of my energies on those days, I offer them gladly. People have lost homes, families are in crisis; it's the least I can do.

There are other methods for grounding that don't involve equipment. Digging in the garden with my hands and raking leaves with a metal rake that has a wooden handle are examples. Any time I work directly in the earth with my body, it is grounding.

I can also visualize a tree with deep and spreading roots that grow deeper and deeper as they connect to Mother Earth. I use this visualization when I am away from home and feeling "floaty" or am having trouble concentrating. I do some deep breathing at the same time.

Did you know that water helps to ground us? It conducts the messages from Mother Earth right through our feet. Wetting the soil wherever we are sitting or wetting the *unpainted* concrete floor where we rest our feet will allow for added conductivity. Walking in water at a beach or lake edge is what I like to do as often as I can. And it is a scientific fact that salt water is more conductive than lake water (*Earthing*, pp. 100–101).

Earthing has provided me with a great deal more understanding about our health and the necessity for being grounded to the Earth as much as possible.

In Patrick MacManaway's book, *Energy Dowsing for Health*, he explains and demonstrates the health benefits of dowsing. After studying and practicing dowsing for a few years, I find I can dowse effectively for my food supplements. I have found that my body doesn't need the same amount each day. I respond to the input.

I also use dowsing if I'm unsure of a decision I'm trying to make. It's not magic; it's a form of communication. Information is coming from my intuitive sense via my muscles. That's what dowsing is all about. *Pendulum Power* by Greg Nielson and Joseph Polansky gave me the history of dowsing, which I found quite interesting. I like to read about a theory or technique before trying it out so that I understand as much as I possibly can. Then I may contact people who have become experienced with that technique or I may attend a workshop on the topic. Last of all, of course, I practice using that technique until I become comfortable with it.

Since I have become aware of the seven *chakras* from great resources such as *The Book of Chakras* by Ambika Wauters, I give thought to them when I am not feeling well physically, emotionally or mentally. I consider the corresponding *chakra* and give support to where the energy is blocked. For example, if I am grieving or down, the *Heart Chakra* is probably involved. The *Heart Chakra* is represented by the color green. Therefore, I wear green, eat green foods, fuss with my green plants, or dig in my garden. I immerse myself in green. I do all this in addition to taking time for conscious reflection about what could possibly be bothering me. And I improve. My outlook is brighter; I feel positive thoughts creeping into my psyche. I begin to hum as I move around and focus anew.

The *Root Chakra* deals with our fears and also the courage we need to overcome those fears. Since the corresponding color is red, I took a red flower with me while I was receiving industrial strength prednisone treatments during my flare of Multiple Sclerosis. I set it on the stand by my chair and looked at it often. I set my intention that the prednisone reduces the inflammation around my nerves. I held that flower. I smelled it. I told my fear to skedaddle and asked for the courage to endure the future. Relaxing my body allowed it to use its energies to help me heal.

While walking down the trail in the fall, a red leaf catches my eye. I am drawn to it. As I move closer, I ask myself—why this leaf? Why this color? Why now? I reach out and touch the leaf. I gently turn it over, examining it. Red . . . fear? Am I afraid of something . . . something happening in my life? Am I anxious about something?

"Yes, I am," I say aloud. I say the words as I identify what that something is and then I examine the leaf further. It is a red maple leaf with its jagged edges. It's soft, pliable, with the red color deepening to the edges. I receive a sense of surety as I hold that beautiful leaf in my hand, and I know I'll be okay. *It* will be okay. I feel the fear dissipate as if in naming it and listening to Nature, I have dispelled its presence. In its place, I experience a surge of courage. And with that courage I am able to recognize my options or decide if there is anything at all I *can* do about my situation. I feel confidence taking over. And I smile.

The use of Nature's colors is an amazing energy for me to be aware of. Color is everywhere—a gift from the Giver.

If I am emotionally upset, I also find that journaling helps me. It is important to be grounded when this happens. A walk in Nature helps me at these times.

Either during or after my walk, I find that putting my feelings into words on paper removes them from me. I can look at them, reread them, even shed some tears of anger or hurt. I become outside of the situation that caused the emotion and can view it in a new light with maybe a new perspective. The hurt or anger hasn't disappeared totally, but it *has* transitioned to a new level. I am not *as* angry or *as* hurt. Sometimes I can even see why things happened as they did and where the other person or persons were coming from besides my own personal perspective. But sometimes not.

Still, the emotion becomes quite modified through the act of journaling.

At times I am helped by writing a letter to the person I feel is the cause of the negative emotion. I write everything I want to say to that person and then put it aside. I let a few days pass, and then I reread the letter. I have written many a letter of this type in my life and never mailed a one. Sometimes I do the same thing by journaling my thoughts and feelings. Saying everything I want to say on paper gets the emotion out of me, and that is the first step to healing my reaction to the situation.

At times, a confrontation may be necessary and actually recommended, even for someone like me, who is quite introspective. Being confrontational does not mean posting blame on the other person. I have found that a good way to begin is, "I felt hurt when I heard _____."

Years ago, I was told by another that a good friend, whom I had confided in, had made derogatory comments about me. I was crushed; I felt betrayed. So I journaled about my feelings. It helped. But this time it didn't bring me the relief I was seeking. I agonized within and distanced from that so-called friend.

Eventually, I realized that I had to confront him and find out why he had spoken so ill of me. However, it took me *two* years to realize and actually *act* on what I knew I had to do. So I made an appointment and traveled to see him.

As I calmly and respectfully retold my saga, his sincere shock was evident. Not only did he deny ever having *said* those things, but he sincerely assured me that he never *would* say those things about me. I floated out of his office, freed from the five-ton boulder that had been crushing me for all that time.

I learned many things from that experience. One was not to avoid or ignore a confrontation if I felt I needed to go that route. The other was not to be so ready to believe negative reports that are handed to me. I needed to trust more, believe in myself more.

Other people might see or hear things differently when something is shown or told to them than what actually was intended, depending on their own emotional state at the time. And people may have their own agendas, their own issues they are attempting or not attempting to deal with.

In this case, what was the purpose for telling me gossip that could only hurt me? I wondered about that.

When we confront someone, we need to be clear about what our intention is. Is it to wreak revenge or to obtain resolution? We need to think about what the consequences of the confrontation might be and whether the worst-case scenario is one we feel we could live with. We need to be honest, sincere, and respectful as we state our case. If we feel we could walk away at peace within ourselves no matter what their response is, then it is worth the risk.

Resolution is not a guarantee. It is *their* choice to accept what we say or not. But *our* stress will be much relieved. We rescind our ownership of the incident.

What is important is what we do with that energy—that hurt, that anger. What do we *need* to do with it? If we're introspective, we might journal, write a letter, cry, or take a walk in Nature. If we're usually confrontational, we might yell, punch a pillow, do some grueling exercise, or take a walk in Nature.

Nature is always there to bring us back to a place of balance, to help us get the emotion out of the way so we can see the best action to take, if any. Nature is our neutralizer, our mediator, if you will.

And she is wisdom.

Rocks, metal, soil, natural materials such as animal hides, silk, cotton, and wood all provide a natural connection with the earth. Spending hours each day grounding ourselves will keep our connection going. We will be more relaxed, more balanced, and better able to handle our emotions.

Happy Grounding!

8

VOICES OF NATURE

In wildness is the preservation of the world.
—Henry David Thoreau

What will I discover as I walk along my path today? I wonder. Will the raven scare me with its loud, sharp, and guttural croak, or instead will I see a deer, gently and cautiously meandering through the forest?

The day is dreary. The gray sky looms above me like one big hovering cloud. The air is still. *The calm before the storm?* I wonder. The air temperature is mild, in the sixties, and a light rain has fallen during the night, dampening everything.

As I pass the maple trees, I notice the water droplets still clinging to the leaves, hanging on for dear life until they either vaporize or are shaken loose, not knowing where they will fall or what they will strike on the way. The leaves seem to glisten from the moisture even though the sun is hidden from view.

I stop and close my eyes, listening as a gentle breeze stirs the moisture-laden leaves as it passes through. The droplets tumble from one leaf to another with a tinkling sound that I find quite soothing. The breeze subsides; I open my eyes.

I continue my trudge up the small hill behind my house. Turning my head to the right, I notice some pink lady slippers, showing themselves in their entire splendor for the first time this spring. There they rest, nestled at the base of some pines, their vibrant pink shade against the rust-colored brown of the pine needle-covered forest floor.

Standing straight and tall, they seem proud to be there, proud to shine, proud to be serving their purpose. *Is it possible these great, sentient beings have any conscious sense of their purpose on this planet? Do I know* my *purpose? Maybe it doesn't matter if I don't. Someday I may realize it,* I wonder. *Maybe I have many purposes at the same time, or maybe my purpose changes.*

Their stance depicts a stretching and reaching to the Light. They need the Light, as we do, to survive.

My deliberation continues. *Maybe I choose my role, and my purpose is much greater—to grow to a point where I am able to love* unconditionally *anyone I meet, without judgment or expectation.*

I notice now that the lady slippers are growing in a cluster of about ten. They seem to be growing individually but not too far away from the others, as if in seeing the others, each gets the support they need. As people, we need the same—not to be identical to anyone else but recognized by others, giving to and receiving from others as part of a community.

These wildflowers are in varying stages of blossoming. Some are at their peak and are a riot of bright pink shades. Others, as they enter their final stage of life, are faded and almost translucent. I think about people. Some shine with happiness—eyes sparkling, faces smiling. Others are saddened and depressed—their eyes are flat, faces drooping. We tend to judge and even condemn them, sometimes putting aside compassion and understanding and replacing it with feelings of superiority. And we all do that—at times.

Many people are somewhere in between the ones who shine and those who seem depressed. We have our ups and downs and try to live our lives without thinking about what long-term effect our behaviors and actions have on others, on our world.

Compassion is the key, the key to loving unconditionally. If we can walk in another's moccasins, as Native American legend has it, we can begin to understand their thoughts and actions better. But do we have to accept those thoughts and actions? Not necessarily, but we need to *understand* where they are coming from. We need to empathize. I believe the world needs more empathy.

Where am I? I wonder. *Where do I fit in this continuum?*

Right now I feel like I'm floating on a cloud. I feel peace-filled. That's what my times out in Nature do for me.

I continue my walk, progressing farther up the hill. There I find two other lady slippers growing tightly together, side by side, as husband and wife. One is taller and one is shorter. Both are in blossom.

Even though they are growing beside each other, they lean apart. *Don't we sometimes grow apart from our partners?*

I move closer, seeing that the taller one is straighter. It is the smaller one that is leaning away. *Is that me?* I ask myself. *Did I* choose *to grow away from my husband, or did that just happen to me on my journey?*

Sometimes life situations, just as changes in the weather, cause one of a couple to grow at a different rate, resulting in the separation. Or is it merely our individuality that is being recognized at that time?

If I were to dig down in the earth where these lady slippers are growing, would I find the roots intertwined? Or would they be reaching outward, searching for a new anchor from which to grow?

Some couples find their way back together, and some never do. In my case, I was being led to a different path.

Having crested the hill, I decide to take a cutoff path to the left. Here, a young Jack pine forest welcomes me.

The atmosphere feels different. The sky is still overcast; the air temperature seems the same. Yet, something has changed. I feel closed in and compacted.

The path has narrowed and weaves through the trees as my feet begin to tread along. I can't seem to lose that feeling of being closed in. As time goes on, however, I begin to become comfortable with the change. It becomes a feeling of closeness and security, even safety. *Maybe it's the darkness that I find hard to adjust to.* It makes me realize that I rely a lot on light for comfort. *I think I need to get more comfortable with the dark. It's time.*

And doesn't this speak to me about how difficult it is to adjust to change? *Especially for me. Maybe for anyone.* I tend to resist change. Familiarity gives me comfort. But we can't stop change; it's always happening. *And I'm all for growth. That's the irony. Growth means change, so I guess I better get used to it. Nature is always changing—it's different every day. What better example do I have?*

I notice that there isn't much underbrush as I move along, making my search for deer trails easier. The deer often frequent this area; I've had many delightful encounters, once with a mother and her two fawns. They walked right up to me and stopped about ten feet away. I spoke to the mother and she looked into my eyes ... how beautiful. Then they meandered on their way.

The encounter made me realize that I am not the *owner* of this land. I am the *protector* of the land and the wildlife that inhabit it. This is *their* home. *I guess I've identified my purpose, or one of my purposes, for now.*

I am reminded of a book I have back at the house, *Animal Speak* by Ken Andrews. He connects our animal totems to some thought-provoking questions we can ask ourselves. If the animal we see appears often, there is a message there for us. Are we willing to spend the time and broach the messages? I have found that it's worth it. It's another way Nature communicates with us if we are open to receive the message.

Since I was having almost daily personal encounters with deer, specifically with one I could now identify, I decided to see what the author had to say about this.

If a deer has entered your life, look for new perceptions and degrees of perceptions to grow and expand for as much as the next five years. It can indicate that there will be opportunities to stimulate gentle new growth increasingly over the next few years (p. 263).

He continued.

When deer show up in your life it is time to
be gentle with yourself and others. A new innocence or freshness is about to be awakened or
born. There is going to be a gentle, enticing lure
of new adventures. Ask yourself important questions. Are you trying to force things? Are others?
Are you being too critical and uncaring of yourself? When deer show up there is an opportunity
to express gentle love that will open new doors
to adventure for you (p. 264).

His words made me aware that I *was* being overly
critical of myself and I sometimes *did* try to make things
happen the way I *wanted* them to. It led me to doing some
serious journaling. I concluded with the commitment to
be gentler with myself and others, giving us all the benefit
of the doubt, so to speak, and to stay open for new opportunities and adventures to arise in my life.

That summer, I was drawn to attend a workshop
called *Publishing and Self-publishing*, being given in Old
Forge, New York, near my home. The presenter was David

Hazard. I found myself attaching to his every word. At the workshop, I became aware that he was going to be conducting a Writing Sojourn there in Old Forge that September.

I have always loved expressing myself in written word and have held onto my dream of one day writing a book, so I decided to take the *opportunity* to attend. Was this my *new adventure* the deer was representing? All those moments of eye contact and communication as the energy flowed between us, all those times I felt camaraderie and bonding between us, was this what I was being led to?

My book was born over that sojourn. It was published in 2016. And now I'm writing another, still on my *new adventure*. How long will it last? Nature will let me know, and I will stay open to new opportunities.

The path is short, and I soon arrive at the edge of the forest. As I step out, I feel an opening up—an unfolding of sorts from darkness to light, from closure to openness, like a bud bursting into bloom. I always have that same reaction here, whether it's a gloomy day or a sunny one. And I've been walking this path for years. I move to my seat, one of my favorite places on the property, where I have a view of the Jay Mountain Range.

As I lower myself to my seat, I find my mind drifting again to the pink lady slippers and what their message is to me about people, about relationships, about compassion and unconditional love.

And I know I have a lot more growing to do.

I can feel myself getting more comfortable with change the more I think about it. If I can look at change as the adventure that it is, an opportunity for new growth, it could be intriguing—a positive thing. I realize this is a reoccurring theme for me, but I do see progress in accepting the challenge that change seems to present—and that's a good thing.

After a while, I arise from my seat and continue on my walk. I wander down the trail and again find myself in a pine and hardwood mixed forest.

Our connection to Nature is seated deep within us. As I meander along, I begin to think about the Celtic Tree Alphabet, or Ogham, as it is sometimes called. It was an Early Medieval alphabet used to write the Primitive Irish language and, later, the Old Irish language. I remember that it dates way back to the first through the ninth centuries A.D., and some scholars even believe it could have been in existence as early as the first century B.C. *That was a long time ago.*

The alphabet itself consisted of twenty-five simple strokes, with each stroke corresponding to a letter of the alphabet and also a particular kind of tree. It has been found inscribed in stone, with scholars feeling the oldest was probably carved in wood, which has long since been lost to the ages.

It seems the strokes or symbols represented a spoken language that came to be recorded as time went on. *I've always been amazed by that.*

As I recall, the first symbol, representing the letter B, was associated with the birch tree. The birch is called a pioneer species, meaning it is one of the first species to take up residence on barren land. This "Lady of the Woods" was a symbol to the Celts of new beginnings. Native Americans used her sap as a source of sweetness. Her leaves were used to treat arthritis and her bark was a natural pain reliever. She protected and she healed, inspiring creativity and hope.

As I find myself thinking more about this "Lady of the Woods," I see a large white birch come into view, standing straight and tall like a sentinel of the forest. I move to her and wrap my arms about her trunk, pressing my body tight to her.

"Heal me in whatever ways I need," I say to her, feeling her energies moving into me. I am aware of a peaceful and tranquil sensation as I breathe deeply, allowing my body to absorb her offering. With a final deep breath, I turn and continue on.

Nearby, I see an oak tree. In the Celtic Tree Alphabet, I remember the oak was associated with the letter D. The Celts thought highly of the oak because of its large size, strength, and nutritious acorns. I can see why it symbolized protection, strength, and stability to them, like a "stick with it" attitude of perseverance at whatever challenges were ahead.

As I look down the path ahead, I notice the myriad pine trees. I remember that pines were associated with the symbol representing the letter A. The tree was a source of vitamin C and used to treat issues of guilt that people might be harboring. The needles were placed in a cloth bag and bath water was poured over them to create a cleansing and stimulating soak. Also, burning the needles, along with cedar and juniper, was used to purify the home. It seems this could allow the attitude of forgiveness of self and others to seep deep into the soul.

Our connection to trees certainly extends into ancient times. They are a common universal symbol that is found in many cultures throughout the ancient world: Shamanic, Hindu, Egyptian, Celtic, Christian. We find sacred trees in many traditions.

The tree has symbolized both physical and spiritual growth in many worlds, in many ways, in many times (www.ancient-wisdom.com/treelore). And its significance and value still lives on today. Fascinating! We certainly do have a symbiotic relationship with trees.

My thoughts begin to drift away from the Celtic Tree Alphabet as I make my way onward through the forest.

A tall tree absent of bark comes into view, pummeled with woodpecker holes. Adorning the gray trunk are bright orange fungi, looking quite regal in their stance as they protrude from their host. The brilliant orange platforms shout of the decay taking place. Yet, I am enthralled by the beauty I see before me. A feeling of deep pleasure radiates throughout my being from my very core. I stand amazed at Nature's handiwork.

My eyes move to the base where I focus on a fallen trunk, butting up to the erect gray remnant of life. The log is covered with richly colored green moss. It had obviously fallen a long time ago, as evidenced by the amount of decay showing—pieces of bark lie on the ground, exposing a reddish-brown interior as it disintegrates to dust.

Colonies of fungi are haphazardly scattered amidst the moss. These glowing yellow curly shaped colonies seem connected, one to another. *What an example of decomposition!*

I recall my readings of Paul Stamets, who describes the beneficial role of fungi and the essential role it has in the healthy continuance of our natural world. I recall its involvement with the cycling of carbon and, of course, the forming of soil. Fungi help in the control of plant and insect populations and mineralize nutrients so they can be used ("Celebrate Decomposition"; Paul Stamets).

Stamets wrote another article about mushrooms, and it says that we are ". . . more closely related to fungi than to any other kingdom." It seems that millions of years ago, we separated and evolved somewhat differently. However, beneficial bacteria are necessary for both of us to help digest food and prevent disease. By growing mushrooms in our gardens, we can neutralize many environmental toxins for they are the prebiotics, promoting the growth of beneficial bacteria like Acidophilus and Bifidobacterium. ("Mushrooms and Mycelium Help the Microbiome"; Paul Stamets).

As I stand there appreciating what I see and marveling at how these beings survive, I realize even more how important they are in the scheme of things. And I know I will never take fungi for granted again or question its role in the health of our world. It is another link in the chain of our survival.

I begin to relate what I am viewing to our aging population of people. What I see before me tells me that aging can be beautiful, too. It does not have to bring images of sickly, shriveled, and crippled people. We can still be supple and loving, joy-filled and compassionate. We can still be a vibrant image of life, just not the same as when we were thirty-five.

My mind wanders back to reading *The Hidden Life of Trees* by Peter Wohlleben. From that book, I learned that tree roots are interconnected, sending messages about drought and danger through their root tips. They even send sugary carbohydrates to ailing or dying comrades this way, and sometimes the fungi surrounding these tips help out in the transference of these sugars. Chemical compounds are exchanged and electrical impulses are transmitted. All plant species in the forest may exchange information this way (p. 11). The author explains Dr. Simard's discovery of the "'wood wide web'". Tim Flannery, in the forward of the book, defines it simply as "soil fungi that connects vegetation in an intimate network that allows the sharing of an enormous amount of information and goods" (p. viii).

I was amazed at the thought of deer nibbling their way down the pathway on their browsing journey. When a leaf is nibbled on one tree, the tree sends a signal via the root tips and the fungal networks to consecutive trees which then respond by releasing toxins into their leaves. These toxins discourage their leaves from being nibbled. This process does take some time. Some trees release chemicals into the air, allowing fellow trees to "smell" the danger and to then release toxins into their leaves. When insects begin to attack a tree, the tree may release a chemical that attracts the invading insects' predator and in that way protects itself from further destruction (pp. 7—10).

I've always felt camaraderie with trees. As a child, I was always *in* the trees—climbing, sitting, and playing. As an adult, I often speak to the trees, greeting them as I begin a walk, stroking their needles or leaves as I meander through the forest, and selectively giving them a spontaneous hug when it so moves me. I have always felt a comfortably close bond with trees, especially the pines.

Resuming my walk, I step on a stone and am reminded that I am barefoot. I love to walk barefoot; that's when the soles of my feet are connected to the earth. I am grounded, whole, peace-filled.

As I continue on, I again feel my mind drifting to the tall gray trunk, swollen with orange fungi. The decay will cause fertile soil and promote new life. And I make a connection to people.

When we die to ourselves—our selfishness and our inappropriate expectations of self and others—we allow new growth through our forgiveness of them, our giving thanks for what we have, our love which we extend to others. It is growth in the spiritual sense.

Being in Nature brings me insight, understanding, and clarity. Spending time with her is always beneficial to me.

Do *you have the time today?*
Do *you have the time?*
Time to be silent
And time to sit,
Or *do* *you have work that you cannot quit?*

Do *you* *have the time today?*
Do *you* *have the time?*
Time to be tranquil
And time to just be,
Or do *you* *have worries you can't even see?*

Do you *have* *the time today?*
Do you *have* *the time?*
Time to be in solitude
And time to be at peace,
Or do you *have* *stresses beyond relief?*

Do you have the *time* *today?*
Do you have the *time?*
Time *to walk,*
Time *to be in the now,*
Time *to choose Nature to show you how?*

I begin to notice all the plants scattered over the forest floor. I sit down on a nearby rock and let the awareness begin to sink in.

Plants have roots, and in those roots the first transformation to food takes place. Plants act as intermediators. They produce oxygen for us to breathe and use our exhaled carbon dioxide for their own respiration. We have a mutualistic relationship with each other.

As our forests are destroyed without replanting, we are eliminating the very air we need to breathe. It causes me to wonder, *Why would anyone do that? What gain is more important than life itself?*

Plants give us the food we eat. They are a major source of nutrition if grown organically without herbicides, pesticides, and chemical fertilizers. They provide us with our vitamins and minerals, our fats, our carbohydrates, and our protein.

I feel better when I'm putting fewer chemicals into my body so it can use its energies, not to try to deal with foreign substances, but to heal itself in whatever way it needs to heal. In my case, the energy went into healing the tissues and rebuilding the myelin that was destroyed during my MS flare. I began eating organically more than fifteen years ago when my daughter began pursuing her degree in Holistic Nutrition.

First I purchased organic lettuce and carrots, adding other vegetables when they became available. Organic eggs and cheese were next with organic fruit. I loved to go berry picking. What's more organic than wild blackberries and blueberries?

Next, I added organic or 100% grass-fed beef, whichever I could find, and organic chicken and turkey.

As for sweeteners, I had used raw honey, maple syrup, and blackstrap molasses for years instead of refined sugar. Eventually, organic cereals, chips, and crackers appeared on the market. I did what I could, as often as I could, to eat healthily, minimizing the chemicals and processed foods.

I began to realize how important it was to buy locally *and* organically. Knowing where the food comes from is paramount to freshness, quality, and taste. The least amount of handling possible is the best. The cost is less and the flavor is incomparable. Fewer vitamins are lost in travel time, so the food is more nutritious.

Over the years since I have begun eating organically, I have noticed that I have more sustained energy, fewer colds, and my spring and fall allergies have gone by the wayside. Mentally, I am more alert and my feeling of a foggy brain is gone. I believe I feel more positive, too.

Fatigue has always been one of the major symptoms of the Multiple Sclerosis I have lived with for more than twenty-five years. I realized, quite by accident, that I am gluten sensitive. This was confirmed by taking the ALCAT test for food sensitivities.

Once I had identified the sensitive foods, I could change things around a bit by eliminating the significant foods for three months. Then I could ingest them every four days for twenty-four hours before refraining again for the four days. This is because it takes four days for the body to clear any antigens it may have produced from eating the sensitive food initially. A food sensitivity is different from an allergy, which can be life threatening. And it works!

So I gave up turkey, blueberries, egg whites, and maple syrup for three months. Now I have them, trying to keep the four-day rotation. With the gluten-containing foods, I do better if I rarely have any. I usually experience extreme fatigue when I overindulge in them or are ignorant of their presence in my food. Fatigue sweeps through me with a wash. I have become quite attuned to the cause.

In reading a book on gluten called *The Gluten Connection* by Shari Lieberman, I discovered that gluten causes inflammation in the body. It may affect the myelin, which is the fatty protective coating around the nerves that helps them conduct electrical impulses to the muscles (p. 42). Disintegration of myelin is what causes loss of function and nervous system sensations in Multiple Sclerosis, so I was onto something.

I've continued my gluten-free diet and am pleased with the way I feel. The less my body has to deal with inflammation, the more it can concentrate on rebuilding myelin if and when it needs to. And the gluten may even *cause* the disintegration of some of the myelin.

There is an amazing amount of gluten in our world today. It is mainly found in the grains of wheat, barley, and rye but is also used to thicken gravies, salad dressings, and sauces. It is used to thicken ice cream, chocolate for candy, chips and bars, condiments, cereals, and crackers. Many creamed soups are thickened with gluten. Even envelope flaps and postage stamps have gluten in their glue.

When grocery shopping, I focus on buying items that are naturally gluten free, have the gluten free symbol on the wrapper, or are indicated to be 100% gluten free. Gluten-free desserts are way too sweet for me, so I make my own. I highly recommend buying organically whenever possible, minimizing the body's need to use its energy to deal with pesticides, herbicides, and chemical fertilizers that are used to grow much of our foods.

When at a restaurant, I always ask if items on the menu are gluten free and, if need be, adjust my order, knowing that bread, pasta, salad dressings, soups, sauces, condiments, and desserts are the biggest culprits there.

I search for the "gluten free" symbol or "100% gluten free" on the label of any packaged or canned items I buy. There are gluten-free ice creams and chocolate on the market, so the searching is worth the effort. Many gluten-free foods can be found in health food stores, but many have a greater amount of sugar or fat, so I try to be selective in my choices.

I remember my brother-in-law's response when I told him what I had read about gluten and my symptoms of MS: "Maybe you don't even have Multiple Sclerosis."

My response to him was, "Whether I have MS or not, I still live with the symptoms every day of my life."

Now that has changed.

After identifying and healing many of my emotional traumas, the details of which I shared in my first book,

My Journey To Wholeness, I was ready to tackle any alternative ways I could find for supporting my body on its journey of healing.

I had retired from teaching school, realizing my body was burning out bigtime. My Zero Balancing practitioner, Dan, referred me to a holistic medical doctor and acupuncture practitioner in Lake Placid to give me additional support for my thyroid and adrenals. My greatest symptom then was fatigue. I found the Zero Balancing was helping me tremendously, but he thought that acupuncture could also be of benefit.

I realized that I was open to trying anything that was recommended by a person I trusted. And I trusted Dan. I have found that a combination of both Zero Balancing *and* acupuncture works well for me.

Acupuncture helps by removing blockages so that the chi can flow better, unimpeded. If I have pulled or strained a part of my body, acupuncture can help by decreasing the inflammation and thereby increasing the flow of chi. I feel better and my body is more able to work on healing the injured part. It also helps when I'm feeling ill; I have experienced immediate relief. I have found that acupuncture provides support for my adrenals and thyroid, allowing my energy to flow more consistently. I do not have to use it up enduring pain and discomfort, nor do I have to use it up to fight off the beginnings of a virus.

Chi is a natural energy that flows through each of us. I'm so glad I have been able to tap into its freeing and consequently healing effects through both Zero Balancing and acupuncture.

Previously, I had thought of Nature's healing energies as being *outside*—in the woods or on the shore of a lake, at the edge of a stream or sitting on a rock. Slowly, I began to realize that Nature's healing energies flow *inside*, also. And each one of us has those within us. Tapping into them brings amazing results.

We *are* a part of Nature!

NATURE'S BREATH

I walk down the gravel road toward an abandoned state campsite, depleted now of all campers. It's fall and the area is closed.

The atmosphere is quite still compared to the summertime, when the campsite is full. Then the campers seem stacked, one on top of another. At those times, people are everywhere, and the noise level is high.

Now as I walk along, the quiet seeps inside, so deep I can feel it slip into my bones. The sky is cloudy; the sun is a yellow cat hidden in gray blankets. I can see a bank of dark, billowy clouds approaching from the west. *The weather report did mention the possibility of rain tonight.*

The pines and deeper green spruces are mixed with maple and aspen trees, all of them scattered among the campsites. It looks like brightly colored confetti has been tossed amidst the green of the softwoods.

I look around at the fallen leaves scattered on the ground around me: red, orange, green, yellow, deep maroon. *Only Nature could arrange them so attractively and intricately. The colors never seem to clash; they just blend into one gorgeous array of beauty.*

The breeze off the lake greets me, tossing my hair across my face. I can feel the temperature dropping as the dark clouds begin to move toward me above the nearby lake. I zip up my jacket and reach into my pockets for the lightweight gloves I tucked inside them before beginning my jaunt.

Brightness surprises me right above my head. Looking up to the sky, I realize the sun has appeared from a bank of clouds for a last showing before the oncoming overcast. For a moment, the mountains, forest, and carpet of leaves explode with color.

The wind has picked up.

One lone, white pine tree catches my eye and begins its performance before me, swaying and bending with the wind. I focus on the pine, as the intensity of the wind quickly increases, depicting the strength of the oncoming front. The swaying causes the pine to stoop farther . . . and farther . . . first one way and then the other. I stand there, watching and waiting, but what am I waiting for? Am I waiting for the pine to bend and snap at any moment?

A gust of wind catches me and turns me to another view.

I see a dance of flickering yellow. I realize the performer is a trembling aspen tree. The leaves seem to spin on the axle of their flat stems—spiraling and gyrating—and appear as yellow specks flickering in the sky. Each branch moves like a dancer's arms, in elegant gestures.

A mood strikes me. A sense of wildness and freedom.

I lift my arms, copying the rhythm of the tree. *Why not?* No one is around. Reaching my hands high overhead, I bend my body to the left and then to the right a few times. Next, I lift myself up on the balls of my feet and spin around. I automatically close my eyes, feeling one with the wind.

What a freeing feeling, to dance with the wind. I feel like I am floating—no thoughts, no concerns, no problems.

I am high above the earth, circling and circling, relaxed and free.

I am one with the wind.

The sun disappears again behind a bank of clouds that is mostly gray, but now also darker here and there—the color of a bruise. The wind is a little stronger.

What would we do without the wind—Nature's breath? I try to imagine a sky without clouds, one that is always blue. Weather would never change. There would be no currents of air or change in air pressure. There wouldn't be storms or thunder and lightning. Where would our toxic fumes go? What air would be left for us to breathe if it didn't circulate?

I have dropped my arms and continued my walk to the campground.

What is the healing power that resides in Nature's breath? Free air can be as strong as a hurricane or as soft as the gentlest movement on a hot summer day. I wonder: *I know it assists greatly in healing, but how?*

My mind wanders, back in time, to memories of my dad.

My father was diagnosed with emphysema at age fifty-nine. He had been a chain smoker since age fourteen. That, coupled with a career of inhaling cement dust as part of his working on construction jobs, resulted in his being diagnosed with that terrible ailment.

As a child, I watched him sitting in his white, vinyl-covered recliner, puffing away. The gray smoke would rise and swirl above his head. I would sit and watch it rise, marveling at the patterns it would make as the currents of air shifted in the room. His chair actually turned a golden yellow as the vinyl absorbed the chemicals in the smoke. And then there were the white sheer curtains hanging from the window rod next to his chair; they also yellowed. Mom washed them often, but the yellow tinge never left, sticking to the fabric like glue.

Six years after he stopped smoking, which he did "cold turkey," he had his first attack. His lungs had not healed from the damage of the smoke, and the elasticity of the cells within his lungs had been lost. He declined steadily over the next few years, until the emphysema took his last breath.

Listening to someone gasping for air, for life, is horrifying. I'd never had the desire to smoke at all. I was twenty-two years old. My dad was sixty-six.

As I continue my walk, my mind leaps from memories of my father to thoughts of Dr. Edward Livingston Trudeau, who moved to the Adirondacks in 1876 and about whom I'd read so much. Suffering from tuberculosis, he hoped to enjoy the quiet beauty of the pristine wilderness as he lived out his last days.

He surprisingly found that by resting and breathing in the fresh clean mountain air, he not only improved, but healed. He established what came to be known as "Cure Cottages" in Saranac Lake and the surrounding area. The first one was called the Adirondack Cottage Sanitarium. These cure cottages treated patients of tuberculosis from all over the world.

What does that say about the value of clean air? Isn't that what all life needs? Clean air does help us heal, just as it can help us to remain healthy.

When it comes to our natural environment and the quality of our air, there are great battles to be fought and hopefully won. Nonetheless, there are things we can do to help ensure the air we breathe in our homes is as clean as possible.

In Nature's design, plants release the oxygen we need to survive, and humans release the carbon dioxide the plants need to survive. It's a delicate balance. *Why would we destroy plants without replenishing the supply when they are necessary for our very survival?* Plants not only give us the oxygen we breathe but also work to cleanse the air of toxins in our environment.

In his book, *How To Grow Fresh Air*, Dr. B.C. Wolverton highlights fifty houseplants that work at purifying the air in our homes and offices. By bringing these plants into our homes and offices, we make the air we breathe cleaner, and we also help to relieve our own stress—"improving mental and physical well-being at any age" (p. 20). He charts each plant and the toxic vapors they remove from the air—ammonia, xylene, toluene, formaldehyde, and so on—and bio effluents such as ethyl alcohol, acetone, methyl alcohol, ethyl acetate. He also charts the water vapor emitted by the houseplants and their ability to suppress airborne microbes.

We know that dry air inside our home irritates our nose and throat, especially in winter when we try to keep the cold air out. This increases our "susceptibility to assaults by airborne chemicals, viruses, mold spores, dust and allergens" (p.26).

The phytochemicals that plants release serve to suppress mold spores and bacteria found in the air inside our homes. Research shows that "plant-filled rooms contained 50 to 60 percent fewer airborne molds and bacteria than rooms without plants" (p. 26).

After reading this fascinating book, my house now abounds in houseplants.

And I am growing my own fresh air.

SCENTS AND FRAGRANCES

Nature's scents can be varied in strength,
Both fragrant and pungent are they,
I love them all
So bring them on.
What can we detect today?

What do I do when I am feeling physically disconnected from the earth—like I'm floating somewhere above it? At those times, I don't feel grounded at all. I feel unsure in my decision-making process. I doubt what others may tell me. I feel vulnerable. Physically, I am relaxed, but I'm not linked to anything. That need for connection runs deep.

What do I do when I'm feeling disconnected from people—my family, friends, co-workers? At those times, I feel self-conscious and self-critical. I want to isolate myself, and that desire seems to increase over time. I do not want to socialize. Physically, I am ready to pounce at anything or anyone. I feel stressed, and the pressure around my eyes is intense.

What do I do when I'm emotionally upset and therefore disconnected harmoniously from mankind? At those times, I am unsure of anything I do or say. I wear my emotions. I feel anger, envy, jealousy, and I crave resolution. I seek being alone. Physically, I am nervous and as tight as a bowstring with my muscles constricted.

What do I do? I turn to Nature and allow her to give me perspective and again set my priorities straight in my mind. If possible, I venture outside and breathe in her scents.

It's autumn, and I find myself kicking dry leaves as I walk down the path behind my house. How automatic it is to be doing this in the fall. Kicking up the leaves releases even more of the special scent I connect with this season, one that's hard to describe. It's a crisp smell of dry, dead leaves, fragrant yet pungent. It holds the promise of a time with little fragrance that is quickly approaching. The scent becomes stronger when dampened by rain. It's a pleasant smell of decaying life, part of Nature's necessary cycle, from which new life will sprout. I love it.

It's well known that scents can conjure up memories, and, moreover, that they can be used in therapy for those with impaired memory to evoke important events of the past.

For me, the scents of fall bring back memories of childhood. I used to rake big piles of maple leaves and then run and jump in them, letting the red, orange, and yellow colors fly where they may. I loved feeling them scratching and tickling my face as they took flight. I'd swing my arms all around and scoop up big armfuls and throw them into the air. Closing my eyes, I could feel them land on my arms and in my hair. Then I'd stand up, shake myself till they all fell off, and climb out of the squashed pile. Grabbing my rake, I'd start all over again.

Other times, I'd cover myself with the leaves, their scent filling my nostrils, my mind, and my soul. I was content, balanced, drifting with the clouds in the sky. With my eyes closed, I could imagine I was floating high above, looking down at my world below.

Fall is my favorite season. Its scents give me deep feelings of joy. It's a time of calming down after a vigorous summer of activity. It is a time of affection and closeness with family as holidays approach and a time of anticipation as the natural world seeks to protect itself with the covering of snow. The scents raise a sense of connectedness as if there's something greater than me as the forests close down with a final splash of color. The chorus of crickets chirping fills the air, and daylight hours lessen.

My body seems to soak up the warm, sunny days of fall in preparation for winter's colder temperatures. A foreboding of the starkness and darkness of winter is in the air.

Winter's scent is crisp and cold. It speaks to me of stillness. The frozen air seeps into clothing and makes me want to wrap up to keep warm. My nostrils stick together, and my breath becomes visible on the exhale.

And I wonder why I'm out here in this freezing, blowing snow. My fingers are going numb, and my nose is running to keep warm. What do I hope to find?

Winter's scent raises a sense of bracing and determination: I will get through this. I will plow through until spring. I feel a contraction, a pulling in of blood flow to protect my inner core. My muscles also feel contracted and tightened as my whole body stiffens against the cold. I stop and inhale deeply. And then I know that I am out here to breathe in the scent of the day, to fill my lungs with—crisp, cold, biting, yet invigorating and rejuvenating —air.

The scent of winter inspires memories of tobogganing down the neighbor's hills, building tunnels in snowbanks at the edge of our driveway, and making snowmen with sticks for arms and ice balls for eyes. Each morning, I would awaken and run to the window to see if the snowman was still there where I had left him the day before. I would either be happy at the sight of him or saddened as I watched him melt away.

Playing in the snow— sitting in it, lying in it, rolling in it—were all activities where I was connecting with Mother Nature. I felt safe and secure as I sat inside my cave in the snowbank. It was quiet in there. It calmed me. And I could sit and dream.

The scents of winter trigger a feeling of constriction and withdrawal in my physical body. I want to store up energy for my adventures outside. Being outside in winter requires more calories due to the cold; keeping warm is paramount. The outside cold temperatures, if I am properly dressed, are invigorating and give me a good solid feeling.

The holidays bring the enticing aromas of pumpkin and baked apples. Then comes a time of recuperation and rest. Emotionally, winter's subtler scents are calming and quieting, a time to curl up by the fire at the end of the day.

The desire to walk among the first snowflakes as they begin to drift down is an emotional high for me. And trudging through the fallen snow, feeling the weight of it on my boots while the vision of white sparkling diamonds greets my eyes, is a delight.

And even in spite of the fingers that may become numb and the cheeks that may feel frozen, I'll come out again in the cold blowing snow. I'll buffer the gale-like winds. Because now I realize why I'm out here.

I'm out here to breathe the scent of the day, no matter what the season.

Winter gives rise to spring.

The scent of spring is of newness—fresh, clean, alive—as plants burst forth from the ground and trees bud and flower. I feel an awakening inside of me, too. My lungs open, my breathing deepens. My energy surges and my muscles fire as my step becomes lighter, friskier, and quicker paced. Spring's scent raises a sense of looking forward to the future days ahead.

We can hear the gurgling of streams as they receive the melt of winter's snow. There is optimism in the air in spring. Hope is very much alive. Everything speaks of energy—seeds sprout, buds open, and leaves appear. *Let's get on with growing.*

Spring brings memories of mild temperatures and springtime showers. Walking in the rain is still something I enjoy doing. There aren't many people about. It's quiet and calm. I feel renewed walking in the rain. I love to feel the raindrops falling on my hair, and splashing in puddles is still a delight.

Anticipation abounds for the forthcoming summer, and my mind fills with ideas and plans. I'll soon be burning up those extra calories stored during winter's time of quiet.

What is that sound? Looking up, I see geese returning up north from where they've been wintering farther south. They fly in that amazing V shape, while their honking fills the air. If you watch closely, they seem to continually rotate positions. *I wonder if that is so no one gets tired out from being in the lead.* People can take a lesson from that—share the load, take turns; we are all in this together.

The scent of summer quickly triggers thoughts of days filled with sunshine and warmth. Flowers are blooming and plants are growing, awaiting the harvest. Countless smells fill the air.

The scents of summer raise a sense of steady calmness. There's a settled consistent energy within my body, a leveling out or constancy of energy and muscular function. All is on course, as it should be. As the multitude of fragrances is released, my lungs open up and fill deeply. When I get hot, as temperatures rise, I sweat. My heart beats faster and my breathing quickens. Summer is here.

Balsam poplar trees exude a fragrance all their own, which makes me stop and sniff. It catches me unaware every time. "Okay, where are you?" I plead to the tree. I finally find it after searching high and low. "There you are, standing so straight and tall."

"Gotcha!" it seems to say.

Chuckling, I stand still and close my eyes. I breathe deeply, absorbing this particular scent as if Nature expelled it just for me. I give thanks. Then I continue on my way, smiling to myself. I feel happy and proud, as if I've solved a great mystery.

Each type of wildflower has its own distinct scent, some more appealing than others. As bright and happy as their blossom is, I find dandelions to have quite an offensive smell. Inhaling their fragrance, however, wakes me up mentally, and I feel more alert. I enjoy the array of bright yellow, as do the insects drawn to them, and I have read recipes involving dandelion greens, so they even have benefits when eaten.

Wild roses, for example, look *and* smell wonderful, attracting insects for pollination by both their color *and* odor while others just use one or the other to attract the insects. The roses carry their fragrance for a few days until their petals fall, their beauty being short-lived. When I smell the rose, I feel a sense of joy, as if the scent is being transferred and absorbed into my very soul.

The common mullein, on the other hand, is fragrant only when the bud first opens. After that there isn't any smell to the beautiful yellow flower that lingers on its tall stalk. Bud after bud opens in turn, but you have to be quick to get the scent. The buds never seem to open all at once, so the scent doesn't fill the air like in the case of milkweed.

The full pink blossoms of the milkweed exude their fragrance for quite a while before they dry and turn brown. I drink in the smell and sigh; the sweetness is like no other. I find it both relaxing and calming.

I have kept a log of the wildflowers living on my property and their particular habits and characteristics. Taking photographs of them keeps their beauty alive to be appreciated throughout the winter months when the world is wrapped only in white.

Summer speaks to me of thunderstorms and of the scent after the storm has rolled on. Again, it is distinct and different from any other, being caused by the ozone released during the storm. I allow a feeling of relief and calm to sweep through me after the rain, as everything is cleansed and watered. My whole body relaxes, tension eases, and my blood pressure drops.

Walking after a rainfall energizes me. I feel refreshed, as I'm sure the plants all do. Remembering that our bodies are mostly water, I feel as if I've been watered, too. Maybe that's why I love to be out in a warm rainfall and feel the rain falling upon my skin.

As the clouds roll by
And the sun peeks out
What do you think I do?

I look at the sky
And wonder why
I feel as good as I do.

Scents can trigger positive responses of our mind, emotions, and physical body. They can elicit a feeling of excitement and happiness, lifting our spirits as well as our step. Scents can help us to recall pleasant times and make us smile.

Scent can be for us a healing gift.

HOW ARE NATURE'S SCENTS THERAPEUTIC?

We can use Nature's scents in meditation. The scents can help to create pleasant associations and distract us from stressful thought patterns to more blissful ones. Think of how the scent of lilacs makes us feel. These scents can be subtle and light.

Scents are used in actual healing modalities. The field of aromatherapy is vast in its healing potential. I have found *The Book of Massage and Aromatherapy* by Nitya Lacroix and Sharon Seager to be a tremendous resource for exploring essential oils and their usefulness.

A few drops of peppermint, lavender, or rosemary in a foot bath will help relieve tired feet, and eucalyptus, ginger, or jasmine are great for stiff muscles. To promote deep breathing, a vaporizer containing drops of lavender,

German chamomile, rosewood, or a combination of these essential oils can be used. And a bath containing some drops of lavender can be a relaxing experience after a long and stressful day. The essential oils may need to be diluted with a carrier oil. It is important to follow their specific directions for use; the details are explained in the text (pp. 30–38).

The authors also explain that "The chemicals in essential oils unlock the body's ability to heal" (p. 13). Not only are the vapors inhaled but they are also absorbed through the skin, carried in the blood and excreted. The oil can remain in the body for up to four hours, activating a healing process that can continue for a few weeks. The oils influence our tissues, cells, and organs, affecting us emotionally and spiritually (p. 14). Many oils are used, not only in aromatherapy but in massage, as well.

My personal experience has been with drops of frankincense. When my brother was passing, my Zero Balancing practitioner put a few drops of the essential oil on some cotton balls and placed them in small baggies. I then distributed them to his wife and my sisters to smell at will, keeping one for myself. We all found tremendous relief of worry and a sense of calmness as we experienced his passing. We used the oil-scented cotton balls frequently throughout the days and weeks following. We all reported a sense of peace and comfort from the scent of frankincense.

The uses of frankincense are many and are worth researching. In the article "Health Benefits of Frankincense Essential Oil" on the website Organic Facts, it is stated that frankincense acts as a sedative, lowering our anxiety and blood pressure. It makes us more introspective. It promotes deep breathing and relaxation, returning us to a state of calm.

This is certainly what I found to be true.

There are other options, also, if we are so inclined to try them.

Many summers ago, I extracted the oils from my calendula blossoms. The moisturizing effect of the oil was beyond belief. I experienced a calming feeling of peace when I used the oil.

We also can benefit from flower essences. In *Energy Dowsing for Health*, Dr. Patrick MacManaway states, "There is a philosophy that our natural environment has and always will provide us with everything that we need to restore and maintain our health in body, mind and spirit" (p. 34).

He refers to a Dr. Edward Bach, who turned to flowers for remedies for psychological and spiritual imbalances, which he felt were the cause of all illness. He focused on the vibrational character of each plant's flowers. The vibrational qualities of the blooms were released and transferred to water when they were soaked for a few hours on a sunny day. Then drops of the water could be taken and drank.

The essences work by affecting our subtle bodies, mainly the emotional body. The result is healing and balancing our physical body through a spirit-mind-body connection (p. 34).

I made flower essences from wild white daisies and yellow pansies one summer. I used dowsing to determine whether I would benefit from taking the drops on my tongue each day. I found I experienced an emotional calmness throughout the summer. I felt an uplifting and bright mood from each, an energy I welcomed as I sought to aid my MS symptom of fatigue.

We can use Nature's scents at home and at work to create a healing atmosphere. In the workplace, we can open a bottle of an essential oil and place it in our space, allowing the fragrance to dissipate around us, or we can place a few drops on cotton balls and inhale the fragrance from time to time to gain benefit. There are also necklaces that act as infusers. I have seen heart-shaped pendants on a chain, and any scent can be placed inside and worn as part of one's accessories.

In our homes, we can burn candles that have been infused with essential oils or flower essences to create a healing atmosphere. Balsam pillows can be placed at will. And balsam-filled draft dodgers can reside on window sills and at the base of doors.

Nature's scents surround us. They imbue us with their healing effects. Let them restore us in body, mind, and spirit. Drink in the varied fragrances that Nature provides for us. And heal.

11

A NEW BEGINNING

The art of healing comes from Nature
—Paracelsus

I have found a path of natural, gentle healing. The pathway began in the out-of-doors and has traveled within, to the center of my soul.

Many know of what I speak. Some have yet to understand. I write to express what I know, from my own experience and what I have learned from others, about the role of our great ally in healing.

Here are some of the attributes of Nature I have learned to count on in my healing journey.

Comforting

When I'm hurting, Nature gives me comfort and solace. Her spirit calms me and helps me to focus. I feel enfolded in her waiting arms. And she is *always* there.

Patient

Nature is patient as I tell her my troubles. She listens intently and accepts my view on things, neither agreeing nor disagreeing; she does not take sides. She seems to nourish me with her love and support as she guides me in her wisdom to see the benefits of possible forgiveness, neither blaming myself nor others for my predicament. She acts as mediator. She does this with a gentle, cleansing, uplifting presence. I feel my negatives neutralize and dissipate the more time I spend with her.

Accepting and Fluid

Nature's spirit does not pass judgment. She is fluid, changing day by day, with new experiences for us to demonstrate her wisdom. She persists in her lessons; complacency knows no place in her realm. Rigidity is not her quality; flexibility is, urging me to be flexible in life, as well.

Grounding and Enduring

Her spirit is enduring and grounding. She is as inconspicuous as the clump of moss hidden under the rock ledge and as conspicuous as the orange sunset. She is a great equalizer, bringing a sense of balance in the importance of all creation. When I seek her out, she seems to modify the intensity of my emotions and helps me to see my priorities realistically. I gain a new perspective on things, a healthier perspective.

Challenging

Nature provides us with challenges, encouraging us to overcome our fears. And with the strength we gain by overcoming those fears, we can accomplish things we never thought we could.

Accepting All

Mother Nature shows no favoritism of one aspect of her creation over another, one species over another. Each is as important as the other and both are needed for the whole to be healthy. Each has value; each has its place; each has its purpose. And the health of each affects the health of the other.

Self-healing

Nature can reclaim herself; she can rebuild in her own time. There is no rush. Her pace is slow but steady, constant, and consistent.

Free to Be

She has no obsessions or addictions. Nature does not cling to anything, nor does she need to. She just *is*. We can all take a lesson from that.

Nature, then, is not only our ally—she is our Great Teacher.

We need only take the time or *make* the time to listen to her message. She is speaking to us through her example. Watch ... observe ... let her enter into you and become a part of you. The answer is there. Healing is there.

PROMISES IN NATURE

Healing is there for you in Nature, as you breathe her clean invigorating air, drink her pure refreshing spring water, feel her wispy breath as it moves across your face.

Healing is there in the companionship of Nature. As you go out and visit her, notice how she moves, how she works, and how she gives support, not often in an obvious

or dramatic way, but more frequently in quiet and unob-
trusive ways.

Healing is in Nature, when you take her into your
home, carry her with you and keep her close to you. She
is alive and has a presence. At a seminar I attended given
by Alverto Taxo, he told us that every natural thing we see
"is a different presentation of the same life force".

Healing is in her life force, which she freely offers.

What we need at a most basic level when we are struggling, when we are sick or injured—what we are *searching*
for is right outside our door.

As you allow Nature and her energies and presence
to enter into your life, you find a gentle but stalwart ally
to help assist in your sense of well-being and, perhaps,
in your healing, too. I have also found in Nature a great
sense of companionship, a realization that you and I—all
of us—are one with a force that offers us health. I have
seen that as I gaze at the Full Moon's circle, shimmering
in a clear, darkened sky. I have *heard* that in the gentle
stirring of the wind as it moves through the white pines.
I have *felt* that as I stroked the silken softness of a bird's
feather. I *know* that, with all the wisdom my experiences
have lent me.

HOW DO WE KNOW?

Science has come a long way in confirming the mind-body connection. In her book, *Molecules of Emotion*, Candace B. Pert, Ph.D., tells of her groundbreaking journey into discovering the opiate receptor and where further research has led her, finally giving more credence to the interconnectedness of our consciousness, body, and mind.

From her work, I understand that every cell in our body is covered by millions of receptors. Each type of receptor vibrates at a specific frequency and therefore attracts specific substances to it. This can result in a change in the state of the cells. There can be behavioral changes, changes in physical activity, and even changes in our emotions. Our nutrients may be better absorbed or not, based on the health and tuning of these receptors. When we are emotionally upset, our digestion and consequential absorption may be affected. Over time, dis-ease may enter the picture.

We know that endorphins released in the brain can relieve pain and also cause our emotional excitement. Pert tells us that the opposite may also be true. Our state of mind can also result in this release. It's a two-way street. This is where our ally and Great Teacher enters in.

Being in Nature eases our mind, our worries, and our stresses. We feel calmed and filled with peace. It would seem that because our mind is more at ease, we're releasing more endorphins and experiencing less pain. It *is* a two way street—a mind-body connection.

UNHEALTHY LIVING

Going about our lives, most of us have abused our bodies through questionable eating habits, overwork, stress, and unrealistic expectations of ourselves. Some of us drive ourselves to exhaustion, and we don't even know why, depleting ourselves of life energy.

What are we really looking for in life? What will make us happy? What will make us filled with joy? Is it finding that special person and living the rest of our life with him or her? Is it having that particular object we've always wanted? Is it living in that special place we've always wanted to live in?

Isn't it peace ... tranquility ... love ... and harmony that we seek to make us happy, even joy-filled?

The secret to having these inner treasures is in *believing* that it is possible for us to attain, that we *deserve* to be happy, to be joy-filled. We deserve these things *just because we do, just because we are*—and for no other reason! Happiness and joy are not states of being we have to earn.

Happiness and joy are our Natural states of being.

Where do we begin? How do we develop a happy, joy-filled life?

Gratitude is the beginning. After reading Alverto Taxo's gem of a book, *Friendship with the Elements*, I begin each day in a spirit of gratitude—*I am happy and grateful now for* _____. I mention aspects of Nature I am happy and grateful for, people who are important to me, body systems that need healing, positive qualities I possess that I have become aware of, qualities of someone else that I admire, and so on. I often do this while I am taking a walk, riding my bicycle, or driving my car. I have found it puts me in a positive mode for whatever the day has in store for me.

Happiness rolls in with a bit of joy along for the ride.

I have learned to begin slowly—one small step at a time. That is key. I need to be willing to step outside my convenient realm of normalcy.

As I began to eat organically, I started with one item and gradually added more to my weekly list. Then I added spring water, understanding that my body didn't need to spend its energy detoxing additives and chemicals. I needed to feed it with clean, refreshing spring water.

My grocery bill might be a little higher, but what is my health worth? Health is one of my priorities, for if I'm not healthy I can't be there for family and friends or even to do things I enjoy on my own. Without health, I can't use the gifts I have to benefit others.

You'll see. You'll like it. You'll want to add another item to your grocery list and then another. That's how I began. And others will follow your example. It's contagious. It works.

I also began to consciously channel any negative emotion—anger, fear, frustration—by taking a walk outside in Nature, if I can. Remember those endorphins? I want to get them moving. If I can't go outside because of the weather, my work schedule, or the time of day, I take a walk *inside* by sitting quietly in a chair, closing my eyes, and listening to the water flowing in the fountain beside me, settling me, calming me. Or I can gaze at the picture of a sunrise, a mountainous landscape, or water flowing over rocks.

I might put on that tape of ocean waves washing on

the shore with the constant rhythm they possess, feeling the flow of the waves like I'm being rocked to sleep. I visualize myself sitting on the shore, inhaling the scents of the ocean, feeling the warm sand beneath my feet. Or I might play that recording of Nature sounds—frogs peeping, crickets chirping, birds singing—seeing myself on a forest trail, feeling the pine needles I'm walking on, smelling the scent of the balsam trees I pass. The chickadees are twittering nearby. I stop and listen to them before continuing my walk. And time passes.

I might bring a sprig of wintergreen into my home and inhale deeply to breathe in its scent. I can feel my breathing getting slower and deeper. And I feel wonderful.

Each of us is made up of body, mind, and spirit, all interconnecting. There is interdependency between all parts. And each part must be nourished healthily to maintain its equilibrium. If one part is insufficiently nourished, we can become ill—physically, mentally, emotionally, or spiritually. Yet, if we can retain a state of nutrition for each part, we can be truly balanced—truly healthy—truly whole.

Being in Nature can help us attain that balance, that health, that wholeness. Connect with her and allow her to enter your soul.

We can't change the past, but we can begin anew to affect our present and future. Have heart—it can happen— you *will* feel better. You will have more energy, a more positive outlook, recognition of your personal gifts, and a willingness to discover your talents. You will feel more alive than ever before because you will be living more *with* Nature.

LAYING THE PATH

What do we need to get the most of our healing experiences in Nature? What can we do in preparation?

Sometimes I have a clear *intention*, like setting out in the hope of ridding myself of the anger I feel against someone. Other times, I just want to vent about my life circumstances. Sometimes I need to make a decision and don't know which way to turn. Other times, I just want to regain peace. And then there are the times I just want to *be*, with no other intention in mind.

In each situation, I have found that Nature is there with me in my struggle, or is there just to meet me in my desire to *be*. If my condition is anger or frustration, I speak it aloud to her. Once said, I let it pass out of me. As my emotion recedes, my body settles, and I slow my pace, my mind opening to whatever Nature has in store for me that day. I am open to receiving her wisdom. I'm careful not to have any preconceived ideas about the results of my walk. She is the teacher and I am the student and learning can take time, sometimes a lot of time.

If I am struggling with an issue, I do not want a time constraint. One cannot rush healing; it comes when we are ready.

Nature patiently shows us examples that may help us heal, but do we get her message? Do we see it? She continues repeating her examples over and over again. At times, I am oblivious to her signs. Then, all of a sudden, I get it—a thought, a connection, an inspiration. It all begins to make sense.

And healing begins to occur.

Nature has much to show me, when I choose to spend time with her.

Expectations seem to automatically form in my mind. I must push them away when they begin to cloud the benefits I am getting from my experience. I let myself drift, erasing any negative head talk about what I'm missing by taking this walk or what I should be doing instead. I try to keep my mind clear, not thinking of anything in particular.

I want to be alert to observe what Nature is showing me everywhere I look. I stay in the moment. When my busy mind begins to invade my more wide-open consciousness, I send it away by quickly shifting back to inner stillness and focus.

Openness and focus may come to rest on anything. I stop often and observe. Maybe it's a spider spinning its web, a bird weaving its nest, or an ant moving its egg from a rotted log to a newly dug anthill. What does each tell me?

The spider's web will trap the food which it needs to survive. How does it know how to do it? Yet it does and the construction is strong and intricate and beautiful.

As I watch the spider doing its spinning, I feel a reconnection within me. I am not a loose strand. I am part of the whole and I have a purpose also, as the spider does for the web and, conversely, as the web has for the spider. And I know that *I* am strong and intricate and beautiful.

The bird gathers grasses and weaves its nest where future eggs will be laid. There the hatchlings will live and grow until they learn to fly. How does it know how to do it—to weave each blade so perfectly? Yet it does, and the construction is strong and intricate and beautiful.

Watching the bird building its nest of grasses reminds me that healing comes slowly, step by step. As each blade of grass is interwoven, so are aspects of my healing. Even though the individual blades are flexible and weak by themselves, as they are woven together they become a strong construct—strong enough to support baby birds.

I will become stronger, also.

And the ants—do they ever rest? They seem always busy, carrying grains of sand or transporting eggs. I squat down and watch, amazed. What can I say? They are hard-working, constant, and consistent. How do *they* know how to dig their home? Yet they do, and the result is strong and intricate and beautiful.

The ant shows me that if I persist on *my* journey to show care, that love will give birth and spread far and wide. With hard work and persistence I'll survive against all odds, just like the industrious ant. How can I think otherwise? (While I was teaching at an elementary school, I bought an ant farm and placed it in my science room where we all watched the hard-working ants build their resulting dwelling place. We watched in amazement...we marveled at it all. I think of that every time I see an ant.)

How intricate Nature is, how everything fits together symbiotically, with purposeful flow. And I wonder what *my* purpose is and how *I* fit into the scheme of it all—Nature's scheme. I see myself, maybe for the first time, as an integral part of some great plan, and I know I have a purpose too, though maybe presently I'm not sure what it is. I know in time I shall be shown, *when I am ready*.

If I have five minutes to be in Nature, I take it. If I have fifty minutes, I take it. If I have five hours to spend, I take that. I may come away with an answer to my dilemma or not, but I will have gained an assurance that I *will* find my way.

I want to be careful not to miss anything gained by my time in Nature. I want to recognize how she is helping me cope, how she is leading me.

I need to *feel* her in my body, *listen* to her with my mind, and *allow* her to touch my soul.

We need to cooperate with Nature in the healing of our body, mind, and spirit. And we need to do this regardless of what we may be doing with the help of other modalities—sessions using Tibetan singing bowls, gongs, chimes, drumming, and more.

We cannot overlook what is offered to us *freely*.

I open the door and step outside. The tree lines and hills and sky embrace me. Pausing there, I close my eyes and take a deep breath, feeling the air as it surges into my lungs and escapes in a slow, declining exhale.

I open my eyes and tilt my face to the sky. I feel a fine mist falling as darkened clouds go rushing by. I notice them lightening to shades of gray. A soft wind begins to tickle my face as it dances by, carrying the scent of loam upon it after the nighttime shower.

There is a tone of quiet after a shower—a sense of peace.

As I'm standing there, the sun begins to peek out as if playing a game of hide and seek. I feel its warmth kiss my face as I am bathed in the sunlight.

I sense a cleansing deep within—a brightening of my spirit happening.

After a night of thirst-quenching rain, the earth seems to come alive before my eyes, rejuvenating itself. I see flowers opening and green leaves lifting as they shed their nighttime accumulation of droplets.

My spirit lifts accordingly and the blessings of life—the blessings of Nature—overtake me. I see Nature everywhere and realize I am a part of it all.

"This is my place—my place in Nature—the ultimate blessing of Mother Earth."

I have come to realize on my own healing journeys that no one part of Nature is more important to our well-being than any other. Each is as important as another.

Nature is there—for you, for me—waiting to show us the way. Her energies, her voices are there to heal you—maybe not in the ways you had asked for, but in greater ways she knows you *need*.

Trust. . . .

She knows the way for *you*.

Nature is a marvel,
Her voices guide us all.
They are there, if we but look to see
And answer then our call.

Our call to live and love and be
For each as to another.
Preserve them—soil and water and air
For Earth is our Mother.

EPILOGUE

I awoke in the lean-to and crawled out of my sleeping bag. The day dawned bright and clear with azure skies.

I had wrestled with a painful muscle knot in one calf most of the night. A stiff neck now greeted me each time I tried to turn my head. As I watched him moving stiffly about the lean-to, I could see that Gary, my partner, wasn't doing much better.

We had begun this trip after work on Friday, planning to bed down in a lean-to a couple of hours in. But it was obviously occupied. This one, at Uphill Stream, had been our last hope, which meant we were making camp at 8:30 p.m.—not the easiest time of day to set up camp. We ate the supper we had brought with us and fell into our sleeping bags, exhausted.

We had dozed off until the arrival of the pine martens. These sleek, brownish, and very curious creatures are a little larger than squirrels, with a similar bushy tail. Being nocturnal, they proceeded to be up and about, moving over us and dragging items, such as our guidebook, out of the lean-to. They even spent some time going through our packs. Gary eventually scared them away. But it took effort—a *lot* of effort.

After that we tried to get some sleep, but it was a real challenge.

So now it was a new day. A big day, in fact, for me.

After doing some decent stretching and catching a quick bite for breakfast, we packed up all our gear and proceeded to Gray Peak. We left our main packs at the base of the mountain and took day packs to the top of Gray.

Now we were down from Gray and about to climb Skylight. Fatigue had set in, what with our stress-filled hike in on Friday night and our rowdy companions—the three pine martens—joining us most of the night. But here we were, dressed in our hiking boots, windbreakers, and day packs, preparing to climb Skylight.

My dream of becoming a 46er was about to come to fruition. Skylight was my last one to climb.

The seed had been planted some time before when, as part of an outdoor camping course in college, a group of us climbed Mt. Morris outside of Tupper Lake, New York. The year was 1968.

The experience at the time was beyond compare. The physical exertion was greater than I had experienced in any of my activity classes as a physical education major in college. Besides the physical exertion, the psychological effort of pushing myself to reach my goal and the determination required all culminated in my reward at reaching the summit. I'd had to talk myself through, thinking I *couldn't* do it, wishing I *could* . . . and then knowing I *would*. Sweat and savvy had won me a spectacular view.

I was on an emotional high, but I sensed a spiritual presence all around me, too. I felt enfolded in a gigantic embrace, wide as the Adirondack wilderness with its six million acres of "forever wild" mountains, lakes, and streams. I'd felt totally filled with love—a kind I'd never before felt. The sensation was miraculous.

And I was hooked.

Mount Morris, the peak I'd climbed back then, was not one of the 46 High Peaks of the Adirondacks, but summiting on it was the moment I became aware of the goal that some pursued. People who climbed all the High Peaks were called "46ers." I knew then that this was something I needed to do—become a 46er—*someday*.

Now I was about to climb my final mountain with my soulmate, Gary.

Even though there was still snow on the ground in the High Peaks, the air made it feel like springtime. There was a sensation of cool on my skin; the scent of loam in the air.

We left our overnight packs at a place called Four Corners, where the trails intersected with the trail up Mt. Marcy—the highest peak in the Adirondacks—which we would use to exit our adventure. In their place, we snapped on our day packs for today's climb.

As we hiked through the silent stands of hardwoods that were just leafing out and evergreens with the scars from where the winter ice had broken limbs, the air continued to warm. The blue sky was shining down through the forest canopy, radiant and blue. I felt a bit of warmth arise on my face.

When we reached the base of the mountain, I closed my eyes and took a deep breath. This was it. I was anxious, excited, and I felt energies build within me.

Immediately, the trail began to rise—a little at first, then more. The hard-packed snow on the trail led the way, having been pounded down by the wintertime climbers on snowshoes making their way to the top. It was as if we were on a high ridge. The melting snows had settled into ice-pack, and beneath us, in the forest all around, were hidden waterways. I could hear the gurgling of the snow-melt as it cascaded down the slope right beneath our steps. I crouched to move on hands and feet to make my way, boots digging into the snow.

Step by step.

Step by step.

Sometimes, as the ascent grew steeper, I had to bend down to get a handhold on rocks beside the trail and pull myself up hand over foot.

Gloves protected my hands from the coarse, frigid snow—now, more like sharp ice pebbles—that could scrape and dig into the skin. Still, I set my pace and continued.

Gary kept encouraging me from behind.

Now and then I slipped backwards, but recovered and continued on. My energies waned. I dug deep, deep down inside myself for more and kept going. The long-awaited ascent seemed longer still. I was a child, awaiting a Christmas that had seemed like it would never arrive.

In maybe half an hour, as we rose above the timberline, I picked up a small rock to carry to the summit. Legend has it that if one does not carry a rock from timberline to the summit, it will surely rain. I gazed at the rock in my hand. It symbolized so much for me. I had wanted to experience this day for so many years.

It was not a pretty rock, I noted. Or a sparkling rock.

It was a plain rock, that had been through wind and weathering. Great challenges. Yes. Just like me.

I had long ago learned that being plain could mean that you are so often inconspicuous in a world that prizes flash and physical beauty. But plain does not mean insignificant. This rock was plain as could be, yet very significant to me. It represented my life. It was a part of the Nature I so loved—simple, not showy and grandiose. I had chosen it to symbolize the accomplishment of a dream, *mine*.

The half-mile climb from Four Corners was taxing on me. Very taxing. My shirt was soaked with sweat, my muscles were burning, and my breath was coming in gasps. But with a thousand more strides I had done it. And as I neared the peak, a pile of rocks came into view, created by many who had been here before me.

When I reached the heap, I set my rock on top of the others. Emotion swelled.

Tears began to find their way down my cheeks. I turned to face Gary, burst into tears, and stepped sobbing into his arms. I had accomplished what I had once thought impossible for me.

I was a 46er. MS and all.

A sense of pride, relief, and amazement filled me. Also exhaustion and hunger. But mostly, wave after wave of emotion struck and flooded through me. . . .

Many years later, as I lay in a hospital bed unable to walk, I thought back to that moment of accomplishment, that dream fulfilled.

If I met challenges like that before, I can do it again, I thought. I began to tap into my determination, the same determination that I'd needed to climb all 46 High Peaks, to become a 46er. And I applied it here, to this situation now. That memory gave me the strength to refocus and begin again.

Step by step.

Step by step.

Now, at age sixty-eight, my mountain treks are lower in elevation, and I travel at a slower pace, appreciating everything I see. I take the time to smell the scents of the forest in springtime and in the fall. I listen to the sounds of the birds calling, the brook gurgling, and the wind whispering. I view and take in the beauty that surrounds me *right where I am.*

The smaller mountains are no longer a step in physical conditioning in order to climb the taller ones. They are what they always were—beautiful mountains.

I had missed that.

She walks the world with grace and honor,
She walks the world alone.
She walks the world with Nature beside her,
The mountains she calls her home.

She walks the world through forest and hillside,
She walks the world outside.
She walks the world through valley and streambed,
With Nature as her guide.

She walks her world with the beauty within her
She walks her world inside.
She walks her world as evil confronts her,
She has no need to hide.

She walks her world with simplicity,
She walks her world with love.
She walks her world with generosity,
Wearing kindness as a glove.

She walks her world with humility,
Gratefulness is her creed.
Bringing her light to all she meets,
She walks her world with peace.

LIST OF RESOURCES USED

Animal Speak, Ted Andrews. Llewellyn Publications, 1993.

"Celebrate Decomposition"; Paul Stamets. www.fungiperfecti.com, 2016.

"Celtic Tree Alphabet," www.ancientwisdom.com/treelore.

Comfortable with Uncertainty, Pema Chodron. Shambhala, 2003.

Earthing, Clinton Ober, Stephen T. Sinatra, M.D., Martin Zucker. Basic Health Publications, Inc., 2010.

Energy Dowsing for Health, Dr. Patrick MacManaway. Anness Publishing Limited, 2009.

Feng Shui: The Book of Cures, Nancilee Wydra. Contemporary Books, 1996.

Friendship with the Elements, Alverto Taxo. LittleLight Publications, 2010.

"Healing with the Moon's Energies"; Terry Pippin. www.thewom-en'sjournal.com/2011/10.

"Health Benefits of Frankincense Essential Oil," www.organicfacts. com.

How to Grow Fresh Air, Dr. B. C. Wolverton. Penguin Books, 1996.

"Lunar Sadhana: Why Women Need to Align with the Moon," Monica Yearwood. www.gaia.com/article.

Molecules of Emotion, Candace B. Pert, Ph.D. Simon & Schuster, 1997.

"Mushrooms and Mycelium Help the Microbiome"; Paul Stamets. www.fungiperfecti.com, 2016.

My Journey to Wholeness, Debby Havas. 2016.

Pendulum Power, Greg Nielsen and Joseph Polansky. Destiny Books, 1987.

The Book of Chakras, Ambika Waters. Barron's Educational Series, Inc., 2002.

The Book of Massage & Aromatherapy, Nitya Lacroix. Anness Publishing Limited, 1994.

The Feng Shui Garden, Gill Hale. Storey Books, 1998.

The Five Love Languages: How To Express Heartfelt Commitment To Your Mate, Gary Chapman. Northfield Publishing, 1995, 2017.

The Gluten Connection, Shari Lieberman, PhD, CNS, FACN with Linda Segall. Holtzbrinck Publishers, 2007.

The Healing Woods, Martha Reben. Thomas Y. Crowell Company, 1952.

The Hidden Life of Trees, Peter Wohlleben. Greystone Books, Ltd, 2016.

The Hidden Messages in Water, Masaru Emoto. Beyond Words Publishing, 2004.

The Ultimate EMF Protection; Earthcalm.

Tuning the Human Biofield, Eileen Day McKusick. Healing Arts Press, 2014.

www.mysticbeats.com/The-Chakras.php

www.wiseoldsayings.com

Yoga and Ayurveda, David Frawley. Lotus Press, 1999.

Zero Balancing and Bridging the Mind and Body through Touch; Zero Balancing Health Association.

ADDITIONAL SUGGESTED READINGS

Braiding Sweetgrass, Robin Wall Kimmerer. Milkweed Editions, 2013.

Earth Medicine, Kenneth Meadows. Element Books, Inc., 1996.

Feng Shui & Your Health, Dr. Jes T. Y. Lim. Times Books International, 1999.

Foxey Brown, Charles Yaple. Charles H. Yaple, 2011.

Last Child in the Woods, Richard Louv. Algonquin Books of Chapel Hill, 2008.

Nature-Speak, Ted Andrews. Dragonhawk Publishing, 2004.

Of the Summits, of the Forests, Adirondack Forty-sixers. 1991.

Planning and Planting a Moon Garden, Marcella Schaffer. Storey Publishing, 2000.

Water and Salt the Essence of Life, Dr. med. Barbara Hendel and Peter Ferreira. Natural Resources, Inc., 2003

A NOTE OF THANKS

To David Hazard, my writing and publishing coach, for all your support and expertise. You are Super!

To Peter Gloege and LOOK Design Studio for your diligence in excellence. Your ideas and design are superb.

To Karen Price, my proofreader, for your "sharp eye" in perusing this manuscript. You are very much appreciated.

To my readers (Elaine Baker, Joyce Draper, Cathy Hohmeyer, Kelly Lindsay, Dr. Philip Martin, Irene Riedl, Dan Sullivan) for your insightful and invaluable evaluation of this manuscript. Thank you so much.

To my soulmate and best friend, Gary, who tolerated the discouraging times. I appreciate all the sacrifices you make in living with this author. You provide the solid and loving foundation I need to continue on my healing journey—a true companion.

To my dear family and friends who, after reading my first book, encouraged me to write a second. I couldn't have done it without your love and support.

And, of course, to Nature—forever my guide and trusting companion on my journey of healing. I *see* you; I *feel* you; I *know* you are there. Words cannot express my thanks. . . .

DEBBY HAVAS resides in the Adirondack Mountains of northern New York. There she sees her role as caretaker of the land and protector of the wildlife that abound there. With Nature as her companion, she welcomes her journey of healing and rejuvenation.

Her first book, *My Journey to Wholeness,* is a memoir depicting her childhood traumas and the effects of growing up in a dysfunctional family. When she is diagnosed with Multiple Sclerosis at age thirty-eight, she decides to make some decisions that change her life forever. The results are surprising, even to her.

In this her second book, *A Gentle Path of Healing,* she delves more deeply into the effects Nature has had on her healing of the symptoms of Multiple Sclerosis, the disease she has lived with for over twenty-five years. Now at age sixty-eight, she reveals to us her understanding of the wisdom of Nature that has led her to this point in her life.

A teacher by profession and the mother of two daughters, she brings analogy and insight to her writing, with in-depth descriptions and healing insights for her readers.